DK

LANGUAGE ARTS MADE EASY

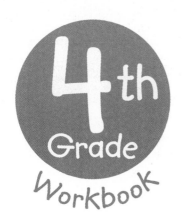

4th Grade Workbook

10 Minutes A Day

Spelling

Consultant Linda Ruggieri

10-minute challenge

Try to complete the exercises for each topic in 10 minutes or less. Note the time it takes you in the "Time taken" column below.

DK London
Editor Elizabeth Blakemore
Senior Editor Deborah Lock
US Senior Editor Shannon Beatty
US Consultant Linda Ruggieri
Managing Editor Christine Stroyan
Managing Art Editor Anna Hall
Senior Production Editor Andy Hilliard
Senior Production Controller Jude Crozier
Jacket Design Development Manager Sophia MTT
Publisher Andrew Macintyre
Associate Publishing Director Liz Wheeler
Art Director Karen Self
Publishing Director Jonathan Metcalf

DK Delhi
Project Editor Neha Ruth Samuel
Editorial Team Rohini Deb, Mark Silas
Art Editor Jyotsna Khosla
Managing Editors Soma B. Chowdhury, Kingshuk Ghoshal
Managing Art Editor Govind Mittal
Design Consultant Shefali Upadhyay
Senior DTP Designer Tarun Sharma
DTP Designers Anita Yadav, Rakesh Kumar, Harish Aggarwal
Senior Jacket Designer Suhita Dharamjit
Jackets Editorial Coordinator Priyanka Sharma

This American Edition, 2020
First American Edition, 2014
Published in the United States by DK Publishing
1745 Broadway, 20th Floor, New York, NY 10019

Copyright © 2014, 2020 Dorling Kindersley Limited
DK, a Division of Penguin Random House LLC
22 23 24 10 9 8 7 6 5 4 3
003–322740–May/2020

A catalog record for this book is available from the
Library of Congress.
ISBN 978-0-7440-3146-1

DK books are available at special discounts when purchased in bulk
for sales promotions, premiums, fund-raising, or educational use.
For details, contact: DK Publishing Special Markets,
1745 Broadway, 20th Floor, New York, NY 10019
SpecialSales@dk.com

Printed and bound in China

All images © Dorling Kindersley Limited
For further information see: www.dkimages.com

For the curious
www.dk.com

MIX
Paper from responsible sources
FSC™ C018179

This book was made with Forest Stewardship
Council™ certified paper – one small step
in DK's commitment to a sustainable future.
For more information go to
www.dk.com/our-green-pledge

Contents

Time Taken

Time Filler:
In these boxes are some extra challenges to extend your skills. You can do them if you have some time left after finishing the questions. Or, these can be stand-alone activities that you can do in 10 minutes.

4

Syllables and Stresses

To make spelling words less tricky, split them into syllables. Let's get started!

1 Count the syllables in these words.

supermarket ☐   gardening ☐   furious ☐

adventure ☐   preparation ☐   journey ☐

2 Link together the words that have the same number of syllables.

color   dangerous   picture   afterward

exhausted   shadow   introduce   outside

3 Look at the pictures of these two-syllable words. The second syllable has been given. Write the letters to spell the first syllable.

............sure

............ent

4 Look at the pictures of these two-syllable words. The first syllable has been given. Write the letters to spell the second syllable.

wiz............

whis............

Time Filler:
Start a spelling journal to record words that you would like to remember how to spell. Write the words that you are having trouble spelling out. Add interesting words that you find from the books you read. Use a page for each letter of the alphabet.

(5) A part of each label is given. Look at each picture and complete its label. How many syllables does each word have?

___ca___ ☐   _____fall ☐   _____tain ☐

(6) When one syllable is longer and louder, it is a **stressed** syllable. Circle words that are stressed at the beginning, and cross out words that are stressed at the end.

demand   restore   forget   table   famous

(7) These words are spelled the same, but have different meanings when the stress changes. For each word, put a check mark in the noun or verb column.

Word	Noun	Verb
record		
re**cord**		
progress		
pro**gress**		

Are the nouns stressed at the beginning or at the end? ....

(8) Write your name and circle the stress. How many syllables are there? ☐

Origins of Prefixes

A prefix is added to the beginning of a root word. It changes the meaning of the word. Try them out!

1 Complete this chart of prefixes that have come from the Latin language. For each prefix, use a dictionary to write two more words, and then work out their meanings.

Prefix	Example 1	Example 2	Example 3	Meaning of Prefix
aqu-	aqueduct			
pro-	proceed			
im-	import			
in-, ir-, il-	incorrect			
pre-	preview			
re-	redo			
sub-	submarine			
super-	superstar			
ex-	external			
co-	cowriter			
de-	defrost			

Time Filler:
How many words, with three or more letters, can you make with the letters in "investigation"? Here are three words to get you started: "vote," "gain," and "sting."

(2) Complete this chart of prefixes that have come from the Greek language. For each prefix, use a dictionary to write two more words, and then work out their meanings.

Prefix	Example 1	Example 2	Example 3	Meaning of Prefix
anti-	antiviral			
auto-	autograph			
kilo-	kilogram			
cy-	cyclone			
dyna-	dynasty			
geo-	geography			
micro-	microscope			
mis-	misbehave			
peri-	periscope			
mono-	monorail			
bio-	biology			

Root Words

Root words are the forms of words without any prefixes or suffixes added. How well can you recognize them?

(1) Complete this chart of Latin and Greek root words. For each root word, use a dictionary to write two more words based on this root word, and then work out its meaning.

Root Word	Example 1	Example 2	Example 3	Meaning of Root Word
dict	dictate			
pel	repel			
scrib	describe			
tract	attract			
vert	divert			
ject	eject			
chron	synchronize			
path	sympathy			
phon	telephone			
gram/graph	diagram			
scope	telescope			

Time Filler:
A useful way to learn spellings is to find complete words within words. For example, remember the spelling of "definitely" by finding the word "finite" within it. Can you find complete words within these words: "fortunate," "emigrate," "apparent," and "correspond"?

(2) The following words are French in origin:
Words with "sh" sound spelled **ch**, such as "chef;"
words with "g" sound spelled **gue**, such as "tongue;"
words with "k" sound spelled **que**, such as "unique."

Words with "s" sound spelled **sc**, such as "science," are Latin in origin.
Words with "k" sound spelled **ch**, such as "chorus," are Greek in origin.

Say each of the following words aloud, and then write them under the French, Italian (Latin), or Greek flags.

chauffeur	chemist	fascinate	scissors
school	scene	chalet	antique
character	league	anchor	muscle

French   **Italian (Latin)**   **Greek**

Spelling Suffixes

Our language is full of suffixes
that are added on to the ends
of root words. The suffixes
suggest a state of being.
Are you ready to try these?

(1) Complete this chart of common suffixes. For each suffix, use
a dictionary to write two more words based on this suffix, and
then work out their meanings.

Suffix	Example 1	Example 2	Example 3	Meaning of Suffix
-ship	membership			
-hood	childhood			
-ness	kindness			
-ment	enjoyment			
-less	helpless			
-dom	kingdom			
-some	wholesome			
-craft	handicraft			
-ology	biology			
-ward	downward			
-ism	criticism			

Time Filler:
Another useful way to know the spelling of tricky words is to learn a phrase that uses the letters in order. For example, for the word "geography," remember: Greg Egg's Old Grandmother Rode a Pig Home Yesterday. Make your own phrases for words that you find tricky to spell.

2 Make words by combining each word with one of the suffixes: -**ness**, -**ment**, or -**ship**. Remember: If the word ends in a consonant + **y**, change the **y** to an **i** before adding the suffix.

silly .... agree .... drowsy ....

merry .... partner .... close ....

3 More than one suffix can sometimes be added. Write these words.

fear + some + ness = ...

care + less + ness = ...

4 When the root word ends in **e**, the final **e** is dropped before adding the suffix. When the root word ends in **y**, the final **y** is dropped before adding the suffix. Complete the words in the chart with the vowel suffixes -**ive**, -**ic**, or -**ist**.

Suffix -**ive**	Suffix -**ic**	Suffix -**ist**
respons............	horrif............	violin............
act............	terrif............	special............
decorat............	histor............	art............
narrat............	allerg............	journal............

"le" Sound

There are a number of spelling
patterns that make the "le" sound.
These are mostly a combination of
two letters: a vowel + the consonant **l**.

1 The most common spelling of the "le" sound at the end of
a root word is **le**. Connect the rhyming words.

settle   wiggle   tumble   buckle

rumble   dimple   kettle   saddle

simple   chuckle   paddle   giggle

2 Other spelling patterns that may be used for the "le" sound are
el or **al**. In a few words, **il** or **ol** is used. Complete these words.
Use a dictionary if needed.

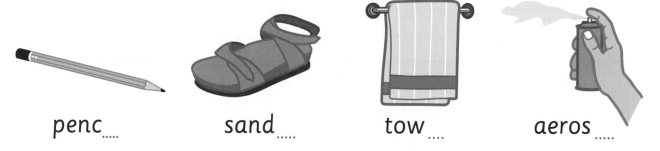

penc.....   sand.....   tow....   aeros.....

3 If the "le" sound is a suffix ending, then use the letters **al**. This suffix
is used when changing nouns to adjectives. **Note:** Sometimes the
spelling of the noun must be changed slightly before adding **al**.

continent + al = ...   navy + al = ...

music + al = ...   nation + al = ...

Time Filler:
Create your own crossword with words that end in the "le" sound. Use a dictionary to help you write the clues. To begin with, use words such as "resemble," "horrible," "festival," "mineral," "miracle," and "punctual."

4 Complete the crossword. The first three letters of each word are given to you. All words have the "le" sound at the end. Use a dictionary to find the words.

Across

1. Having very hot and humid conditions (tro)
2. A celebration on the street (car)
3. A round shape (cir)
4. The remains of prehistoric living things (fos)
5. Furniture you eat at (tab)

Down

1. A human-made underground passage (tun)
2. An item or object (art)
3. A mystery or a game with interlocking pieces (puz)
4. A warm-blooded animal that has fur (mam)
5. A large building with thick walls, towers, and battlements (cas)

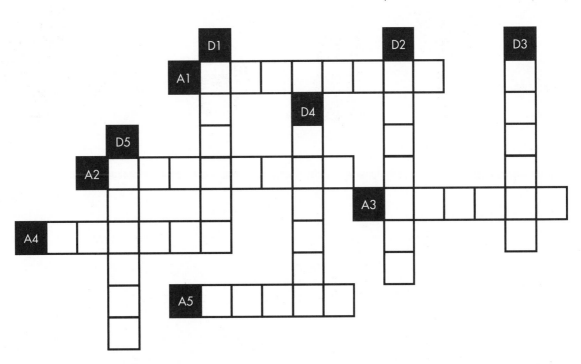

Comparing Adjectives

Find out what happens to adjectives when you start comparing things.

1. Add **er** to words to compare two things (comparative) and **est** when something is of the highest order (superlative). Complete the sentences.

Max   Tom   Sam

Max is fast, Tom is ....,
and Sam is the ....

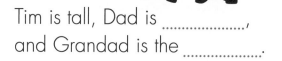

Tim   Dad   Grandad

Tim is tall, Dad is ....,
and Grandad is the ....

2. Write the correct adjectives in the spaces.

Pine

Palm

Apple

The apple tree is large,
the palm is .... , and
the pine is the ....

3. Write the correct adjectives in the spaces.

Great Dane

Greyhound

Collie

The Collie is big, the Greyhound
is ...., and the Great Dane
is the ....

4. For words ending with a consonant + **y**, change the **y** to **i** and add the ending. Use the word "angry" to complete the sentence.

John is angry, Jane is ...., and Justin is the ....

5) For most three-syllable adjectives and some two-syllable adjectives, use "more" for the comparative and "most" for the superlative. Add "more" and "most" to this sentence.

The gardener is knowledgeable about plants. The tree surgeon is .... knowledgeable than the gardener. The botanist is the .... knowledgeable of all the plant lovers.

6) Complete the chart with the comparatives and the superlatives.

Adjective	Comparative	Superlative
slow		
wet		
busy		
important		

7) There are some irregular adjectives that do not follow these spelling rules. Can you link the adjective to its comparative and superlative?

Adjective	Comparative	Superlative
good	worse	best
bad	farther	least
little	better	worst
far	less	farthest

"Not" Prefixes

The prefixes **in-**, **im-**, **ir-**, and **il-** all mean "not." Also, **un-**, **dis-**, and **de-** mean "not" and are used as exceptions. Try these out!

(1) The prefix **in-** is used most often. Write these words.

not direct = ...

not active = ...

not accurate = ...

not capable = ...

(2) Add **ir-** to root words beginning with **r**, making a double **r**. Write these words.

not regular = ...

not responsible = ...

not removable = ...

(3) Add **il-** to root words beginning with **l**, making a double **l**. Write these words.

not legal = ...

not legible = ...

not logical = ...

(4) Add **im-** to some root words beginning with **m** and **p**. Write these words.

not mobile = ...

not proper = ...

not possible = ...

(5) There are exceptions to the above rules. Circle the words spelled correctly.

defrost or infrost

illike or dislike

unload or ilload

irreasonable or unreasonable

depart or inpart

implease or displease

Time Filler:
How many words, with three or more letters, can you make with the letters in "immediately"? Here are three words to get you started: "team," "lime," and "meal."

(6) Find the opposite of each of these root words in the word search.

credible   aware   polite   code   order
accurate   patient   made   compose   modest

i	n	c	r	e	d	i	b	l	e
m	r	i	a	i	e	u	t	n	v
p	e	m	p	r	c	n	i	i	u
a	d	p	r	o	o	m	s	m	n
t	r	o	l	m	d	a	d	m	a
i	o	l	d	t	e	d	s	o	w
e	s	i	e	o	p	e	i	d	a
n	i	t	s	d	i	s	d	e	r
t	d	e	c	o	m	p	o	s	e
i	n	a	c	c	u	r	a	t	e

Changing **y**

The "igh" or "ee" sound at
the end of a word is often
spelled with the letter **y**.
Listen out for them!

① Add the letter **y** to these words and use the words to complete the
sentences. **Hint:** For some short words, double the last consonant.

crisp	fuss	sun	run	fur	full

The bacon tasted ....   The day was hot and ....

The kitten was ....   The toddler was ....

The gravy was ....   The restaurant was ....booked.

② These words end with an **e**. Add the letter **y** to them.
Hint: Drop the **e** to add the **y**.

bone   smoke   stone   grease   laze

....

Why is the **e** removed? ....

③ Circle the words with **y** as an "igh" sound.
Cross out the words with **y** as an "ee" sound.

cry   boy   hurry   stay   happy   apply

What is different about the **y** in the words not circled or crossed out?

....

Time Filler:
Here is a rhyme to help you remember the spelling of "difficulty": Mrs D, Mrs I, Mrs FFI, Mrs C, Mrs U, Mrs LTY. Try this method with the words "similarity" and "tremendous."

4 Can you find 10 words from page 18 in this word search?

h	a	b	m	r	h	o	t	b	y
u	n	o	n	l	a	z	y	m	g
r	u	n	n	y	p	a	l	p	r
r	o	y	u	a	p	p	l	y	e
y	m	g	l	p	y	d	n	f	a
b	f	u	l	s	a	f	n	o	s
p	u	f	z	y	l	u	s	s	y
z	s	m	o	k	y	l	a	g	l
l	s	f	r	m	f	l	r	r	t
o	y	t	g	s	s	y	t	f	m

Useful Word List 1

Read each column of words. Next cover the words up one by one and write them. Then move on to the next column.

Monday	....
Tuesday	....
Wednesday	....
Thursday	....
Friday	....
Saturday	....
Sunday	....
holiday	....
yesterday	....
tomorrow	....
birthday	....
anniversary	....
weekend	....
weekly	....

tonight	....
today	....
month	....
morning	....
afternoon	....
season	....
winter	....
spring	....
summer	....
fall	....
January	....
February	....
March	....
April	....

Time Filler:
Choose five words from this list
and use each one in its own sentence.
Keep coming back to these lists to check
that you still know these useful words.

May	....	seventeen	....
June	....	eighteen	....
July	....	nineteen	....
August	....	twenty	....
September	....	thirty	....
October	....	forty	....
November	....	fifty	....
December	....	sixty	....
eleven	....	seventy	....
twelve	....	eighty	....
thirteen	....	ninety	....
fourteen	....	hundred	....
fifteen	....	thousand	....
sixteen	....	million	....

Tricky Plurals

To make nouns plural,
you usually add **s**.
But for many words,
it is not as simple as that.

1 Add **es** to words that end in **s**, **x**, **z**, **sh**, **ch**, or **ss** to make them plural.

brush ....   glass ....   match ....

2 For words ending in a consonant + **y**, change **y** to **i** and add **es**.

puppy ....   pony ....   city ....

3 Add **s** to most words ending in an **o**.

piano ....   solo ....   yo-yo ....

There are exceptions to this rule. Add **es** to make these words plural.

potato ....   volcano ....   cargo ....

4 For words ending in an **f** or **fe**, change **f** or **fe** to **v** and add **es**.

half ....   leaf ....   knife ....

There are exceptions to this rule. Just add **s** to make these words plural.

roof ....   chief ....

5 For words ending in an **ff**, just add **s**.

cuff ....   sniff ....   puff ....

Time Filler:
Rewrite the following sentence,
making all singular words into plural:
The witch added an eye of a frog,
a foot of a bird, a tail of a horse,
and a scale of a fish.
Write your own witches' potion.

(6) Some words change completely when made plural.
Match each word to its plural.

child   geese

mouse   larvae

goose   children

larva   mice

(7) Some words stay the same when made plural. Circle those words below.

deer   monkey   sheep   fish   cat

(8) Complete the sentences using the plural of these words.

penny	fox	loaf	foot

Jan bought a candy with ten ....

In the field, a fox ran to join the other ....

The baker baked ten .... of bread.

The plank of wood measured six ....

Silent Letters

More than half of the words in the
English language have silent letters.
Many of those letters were pronounced
in the past. Some silent letters were
added in the 16th century to make
words reflect their Latin roots.

1 Circle the letter you cannot hear in these words.

kneel   wrap   honest   rhyme   psalm

climb   half   gnaw   column   receipt

2 Say the word on each envelope. Then write the word in the correct
letterbox below.

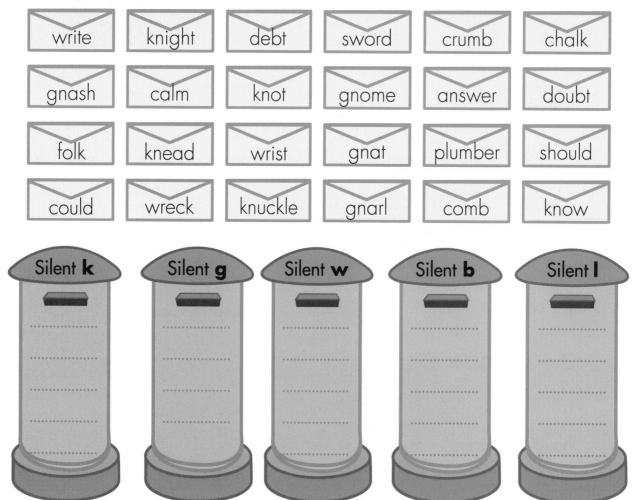

write   knight   debt   sword   crumb   chalk

gnash   calm   knot   gnome   answer   doubt

folk   knead   wrist   gnat   plumber   should

could   wreck   knuckle   gnarl   comb   know

Silent **k**   Silent **g**   Silent **w**   Silent **b**   Silent **l**

Time Filler:
The letter **p** is silent when followed by either **sy** or **n** at the beginning of a word. Use a dictionary to find five words for each spelling pattern. Here are a couple of words: "psychedelic" and "pneumatic."

③ Look at question 2 on page 24 to find the answers.

Which consonants come before and after a silent **b**?

....

Which consonants come after a silent **l**?

....

Which consonant comes after a silent **k** and a silent **g**?

....

Which consonants come before and after a silent **w**?

....

④ Complete each of these words with its silent letter.

 .....nife

40 + 12 = 53 ✗ .....rong

 cu.....board

 yo.....k

 lam.....

 .....onor

Adding -**ful** and -**ly**

Note how each suffix affects its root word.

1. When the word "full" becomes the suffix -**ful**, the final **l** is dropped. Write each of these as one word.

   full of truth = ...   full of wonder = ...

   full of cheer = ...   full of play = ...

2. When words end in a consonant followed by **y**, change the **y** to **i**. (**Example**: pity + full = pitiful, but play + full = playful)

   beauty + full = ...   plenty + full = ...

   care + full = ...   power + full = ...

3. The suffix -**ly** is added to an adjective to form an adverb.
   Note: An adjective describes a noun. An adverb describes an action.

   quick + ly = ...   slow + ly = ...

4. If the root word ends in a **y**, then change **y** to **i**. Complete these words.

   speedy + ly = ...   happy + ly = ...

5. If the root words have a consonant + **le**, change -**le** to -**ly**.

   gentle + ly = ...   simple + ly = ...

   noble + ly = ...   humble + ly = ...

Time Filler:
If you find some words tricky, make a story using its letters. To remember "accidentally" with its double **c** and an **ally**, you could make a story about two cats that accidentally scratched your ally (friend). Can you create a story about a special ally for "especially"?

(6) If the root word ends in **ic**, then add the letters **ally**.
Change these words to adverbs.

basic _____   frantic _____   dramatic _____

(7) In some exceptions, just drop the **e**, then add **-ly** to the words.

true + ly = _____   whole + ly = _____

(8) Complete the chart below.

Adjective	Adverb
kind	
quiet	
	strangely
famous	
	normally
general	

Adjective	Adverb
easy	
	heavily
fateful	
noisy	
	loyally
	readily

Write a sentence using one of the words from the chart.

_____

_____

Apostrophes

Apostrophes are used to mark the place of missing letters in contractions and in words showing ownership. (**Example:** The children found the dog's collar.)

1 What are the missing letters in these words?

it's ......   isn't ......   they're ......

I've ......   can't ......   we'll ......

2 Make these words into one word using an apostrophe.

I am ....   he had ....   do not ....

she would ....   you will ....   does not ....

3 Connect the words with their contractions.

should not   o'clock

of the clock   shouldn't

pick and mix   aren't

are not   pick 'n' mix

4 Rewrite the sentences in the speech bubbles, using contractions.

Time Filler:
Look through a newspaper to find words with apostrophes. Make a list of words that are in contracted forms and those that show possessives. Why do you think the contracted forms have been used?

(5) An apostrophe is put after the owner's name to show something belongs to him or her. If the owner's name is a plural that does not end in **s**, then add an apostrophe and an **s**. Complete these words.

Tim___ dog.   The women___ group.

The dog___ bone.   The children___ game.

(6) If the owner's name is singular but already ends in **s**, then still add an apostrophe and an **s**.

James___ bat.   The actress___ costume.

(7) If the owner is plural and already ends in **s**, then just add an apostrophe.

The ladies__ coat.   The dogs__ collars.

Three years__ work. The two brothers__ cars.

(8) Sometimes contractions can be confused with possessives. Underline the correct word in the brackets for each sentence.

The children visited (they're/their) grandparents.

(You're/Your) going to be late for school.

(Who's/Whose) sweater is this?

The dog ate (it's/its) dinner.

Topic Prefixes

Remembering prefixes and
their meanings helps improve
both spelling and vocabulary.
Are you ready to try these?

1 The prefix **auto**- means "self." Connect each word to its meaning.

autograph   Able to work by itself

automatic   A person's story of his/her life

autobiography   A person's signature

2 The prefix **circum**- means "round." What do each of these words
go "round"?

circumference   circumnavigate

3 These words begin with the same prefix. The prefix means "distant."
Circle the prefix.

telephone   telescope

4 What number do these prefixes mean?

cent- as in centipede   **tri**- as in tripod

quart- as in quarter   **pent**- as in pentagon

uni- as in unicycle   **dec**- as in decade

Time Filler:
Search in science, math, and geography books for more words that begin with the prefixes used on this page. Can you find words in these books that use other prefixes?

(5) Here are some words with the prefix **trans**-. What does it mean?

| transmit | transfer | transport | translate | transplant |

(6) The prefix **bi**- means "two" or "twice." Complete the crossword using **bi**- words. Use a dictionary to find the words.

Across
1. Two-footed
2. To split in two equal parts
3. Occurring every two years
4. Able to speak two languages

Down
1. Muscle with two starting points
2. Two-wheeled vehicle
3. Eyeglasses with two parts
4. Plane with two pairs of wings

Doubling Letters

Spelling a word becomes
doubly tricky when letters
are doubled. Here are a
few tips to help you.

Complete these words following the doubling-letter rules.

1 When adding a suffix that begins with a vowel (**-ed**) to a word that
ends with a vowel and a consonant, double the last consonant.

stop + ed = ...

plan + ing = ...

fit + ed = ...

step + ed = ...

2 Double the last consonant of a word to add a suffix when
the last syllable is stressed.

begin + er = ...

occur + ing = ...

3 Do not double the last consonant when a word ends in
more than one consonant.

jump + ed = ...

sing + er = ...

help + ing = ...

rest + ing = ...

4 Do not double the last consonant when the last syllable
is unstressed.

offer + ed = ...

garden + er = ...

5 Do not double the last consonant when the suffix begins
with a consonant.

sad + ly = ...

power + ful = ...

Time Filler:
Remember the spelling of "accommodate" by learning: the word is large enough to accommodate both a double **c** and a double **m** with an **o** after each. In your spelling journal (see page 5), list words with double letters, such as "occurrence" and "possession."

6 Circle the words where the last consonant will be doubled before adding a suffix.

soak	thin	fast	pack	spot
run	walk	plan	clean	sit
comfort	disgust	drop	assist	forget
color	grab	enjoy	reason	listen

7 In the middle of a word, letters are doubled after a short vowel sound. Complete each word and connect it to its picture.

ra___it   a___le   ca___ot   che___y   pi__ow

8 In the middle of a word, letters are not doubled after a long vowel sound. Circle the words with the long vowel sound.

dinner	diner	super	supper
pole	pollen	written	writing

Crafty Consonants

Some consonants are used
in specific ways in words.
Get ready to investigate
the letters **k**, **v**, and **w**.

1 Say these words with the "k" sound aloud. Does the sound come at the beginning, in the middle, or at the end? Write the words in the chart.

keep   rocket   token   king   back   tank

Beginning	Middle	End

Does a vowel or a consonant go before the **k** at the end of a word?

Write a word that rhymes with each of the words ending in the letter **k**.

....

....

2 Say these words aloud. Does the letter **v** come at the beginning, in the middle, or at the end? Write them in the chart.

village   visit   five   develop   verb   river

Beginning	Middle	End

What do you notice about the chart? ....

Time Filler:
Try saying these tongue twisters very fast:
If two witches were watching two watches,
which witch would watch which watch?
Try this: Katy caught a kitten in the kitchen.
Which tongue twister is your favorite?

(3) Underline the letter string **wa** in these words.

was   swamp   watch   dwarf   swan

wasp   swarm   toward   reward

Describe the sound of the letter **a**.

....

Using a dictionary, write two more words with the letter string **swa**.

....

(4) Write the letter string **wo** in these words.

...... man   s ...... llen   ...... rd

...... rm   s ...... rd   t ......

s ...... op   a ...... ke   ...... nder

How many words with the letter string **swo** are in your dictionary?

....

Does the letter string **wo** mostly come at the beginning
or at the end of the word?

....

Common Endings

The "shun" sound can
be spelled three ways:
tion, **cian**, and **sion**.
Give these a try.

① The most common spelling of "shun" is **-tion**. The root word usually contains a clearly pronounced vowel and is always a noun. Use these root words to complete the sentences below: subtraction, pollution.

The factory caused lots of ....

The problem 9 minus 8 is a .... problem.

② Use **-cian** for the names of occupations. Write these words.

A person who does magic = ...

A person who plays music = ...

③ Use **-sion** after **r**, **l**, and sometimes **n**. Add **-sion** to these words.

ver..........   propul..........   ten..........

④ Use **-sion** where the root word ends in **d**, **de**, **s**, or **se** and for a soft "sh" sound. Drop the root-word endings before adding the suffix to these words.

extend + sion = ...   confuse + sion = ...

discuss + sion = ...   possess + sion = ...

⑤ Use **-tion**, **-cian**, or **-sion** to complete these words.

posi..........   pas..........   physi..........

educa..........   opti..........   mis..........

Time Filler:
Look at the letters on car license plates. Can you think of words that have those letters in them? For example, a license MLD could be used to make the words "melted" and "misleading."

(6) The **-ient** is used after **t** or **c** to make the "shunt" sound. Add **-ient** to these words.

effic........   pat........   anc........

(7) The **-ial** ending is used after **t** or **c** to make the "shul" sound. The **-cial** ending often comes after a vowel and the **-tial** ending after a consonant. Add **-ial** to these words.

spec......   soc......   influent......

(8) The **-ure** ending is used after **t** to make the "chuh" sound or after **s** to make the "zhuh" sound. Complete these words.

moist......   meas......   furnit......

(9) The **-ous** ending makes the "us" sound and is used for adjectives. Draw a line to link each word to its meaning.

anxious   describes a meal that is tasty

ravenous   describes a person who is worried

delicious   describes an animal that is hungry

(10) If there is an "i" sound before the **-ous** ending, it is usually spelled as **i**, but a few words have **e**. Circle the correct word.

serious or sereous   hidious or hideous

Homophones

Words that sound the same, but are spelled differently and have different meanings are called homophones.
Example: The officer wearing the **blue** uniform **blew** his whistle.

1) Connect the words that sound the same.

peace   knot   plain   main   heard

mane   plane   herd   piece   not

2) Write a sentence for each of the words "rode," "rowed," and "road."

....

....

....

3) Put these words into the missing spaces to complete these sentences.

| heel | he'll | heal | too | two | to |

The runner's .... had a blister.
.... need a bandage .... help it ....
The runner had .... cuts on his leg, ...

4) For each sentence, underline the correct word in parentheses.

Turn (right/write) at the intersection.

No one (new/knew) whose turn it was to do the dishes.

I can (hear/here) the birds singing.

Time Filler:
To distinguish between the words "stationary" and "stationery," think of an **e** in envelope and pens for "stationery" and an **a** in cars when parked are "stationary." List homophones in your spelling journal (see page 5) and make phrases to distinguish between the different words.

5) In the table below, write these words next to their meanings.

aloud   allowed   compliment   complement
descent   dissent   pair   pear
principal   principle   medal   meddle

Meaning	Word
Say out loud	
Permitted	
To make nice remarks	
To make something complete	
Going down	
To disagree	
The leader of a school	
A truth or rule	
Two things that go together	
A type of fruit	
An award	
To interfere	

Tricky Spellings

Some spelling patterns
make different sounds in
different words. Watch out
for these letter combinations:
ou, **au**, **ei**, and **ey**!

① The spelling pattern **ou** makes the different sounds in these words: "out,"
"group," and "double." Join the groups of words with the same sound.

trouble   house   found

soup

shout   country   loud

cousin   coupon

boutique   young   route

② The spelling pattern **au** mostly makes an "aw" sound.
Circle the words that make the "aw" sound.

author   pause   aunt   sauce

laugh   haunt   launch

What sound does the **au** pattern make in the words not circled?
Note: This does not occur very often.

....

③ Underline the letters that make the "ay" sound in these words.

vein   weigh   eight   convey   obey

Is the "ay" sound in the words with letters **ey**
stressed or unstressed?   ....

Time Filler:
How many words, with three or more letters, can you make with the letters in "breakthrough"? Here are three words to get you started: "throb," "great," and "grab."

(4) The "ite" sound at the end of a word is mostly spelled with the pattern **ight**, but sometimes the letters **ite** or **yte** are used. Complete the words in these sentences with **ight**, **ite**, or **yte**.

Dan dressed in a wh_____ sheet to give everyone a fr_____.

The computer had one megab_____ left.

(5) The spelling pattern **ear** makes different sounds. Connect the words with the same sound.

appear   near   early

wear

pear   ear

rehearse   bear   Earth

(6) The letter string **ough** is tricky. Write each of the words in its rhyming group.

rough   tough   enough   cough   through   although   thought

bough   dough   trough   ought   bought   though

Rhyme with puff	Rhyme with toe	Rhyme with now	Rhyme with off	Rhyme with too	Rhyme with caught

Useful Word List 2

Read each column of words.
Next cover the words up one
by one and write them. Then
move on to the next column.

accident	....	Earth	....
advertise	....	excite	....
approve	....	extreme	....
benefit	....	grammar	....
bicycle	....	guard	....
breathe	....	heart	....
building	....	immediate	....
certain	....	increase	....
conscience	....	independent	....
continue	....	injure	....
describe	....	inquire	....
dictionary	....	junior	....
difficult	....	knowledge	....
early	....	library	....

material	....	regular	....
medicine	....	reign	....
nephew	....	separate	....
occasion	....	sew	....
often	....	situate	....
opposite	....	strength	....
particular	....	sufficient	....
peculiar	....	sure	....
position	....	though	....
possess	....	thought	....
punctuate	....	through	....
quarrel	....	underneath	....
quarter	....	victory	....
recite		weary	

Verb Tenses

Adding -**ed** or -**ing** to
the end of a verb tells
when something happens.
Let's get started!

1 Most words with short vowel sounds do not change when
adding -**ed** or -**ing**.

help + ing = ...   ask + ed = ...

2 For a word ending in **e**, drop the letter and replace it with either -**en**
or -**ing**. **Note**: Some words may need to have consonants doubled.

come + ing = ...   drive + en = ...

ride + en = ...   make + ing = ...

3 For a word that has a short vowel before its final letter and a stress
at the end, double the final letter and add either -**ed** or -**ing**.

swim + ing = ...   hop + ing = ...

refer + ed = ...   admit + ed = ...

4 For a word ending with a vowel + **y**, just add -**ed** or -**ing**.
If a word ends in a consonant + **y**, change **y** to **i** before adding -**ed**.

cry + ing = ...   reply + ed = ...

play + ing = ...   enjoy + ed = ...

5 For words ending in **c**, add a **k**, and then add either -**ed** or -**ing**.

panic + ed = ...   mimic + ing = ...

Time Filler:
What happens to the words "lie" and "tie" when adding -**ing**? Which two spelling rules are used?

6 Add -**ing** and -**ed** or -**en** to each verb to tell what is happening now and what has happened before.

Verb	Happen**ing** Now (Add -**ing**)	Happen**ed** Before (Add -**ed** or -**en**)
look		
walk		
jump		
write		
take		
shop		
drag		
spy		
carry		
hide		

Soft Sounds

In the 11th century, the French invaders of England introduced the soft "c" and soft "g" sounds into English spelling.

Sometimes the "c" sound is hard, as in **c**oat. At other times, the "c" sound is soft and has an "s" sound, as in fa**c**e.

1 Say the words aloud and listen to the "c" sound. Is it hard or soft? Draw connecting lines.

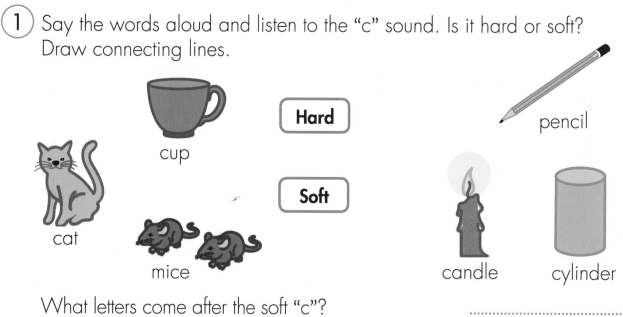

cup

Hard

Soft

cat

mice

pencil

candle

cylinder

What letters come after the soft "c"? ....

2 Underline the soft "c" in these words.

circle   bicycle   circuit   cyclone   accident   circus

3 Say the words aloud and check if the "c" sound is hard or soft.

Word	Hard	Soft
recap		
descend		
cinema		
disco		
cupboard		

Sometimes the "g" sound is hard, as in **g**ate. At other times, the "g" sound is soft, as in ca**g**e.

④ Say the words aloud and listen to the "g" sound. Is it hard or soft? Draw connecting lines.

giraffe   grapes   **Hard**   dog   gymnast

gem   **Soft**   glass

What letters come after the soft "g"? ....

⑤ Say the words aloud and check if the "g" sound is hard or soft.

Word	Hard	Soft
stage		
general		
garden		
Egypt		
gift		
germ		
green		

Irregular Verbs

Verbs that change their vowels
when there is a change of tense
have survived from Old English.

(1) Change these words from present tense (happening now) to
   past tense (already happened). Use a dictionary if needed.
   Look out for spelling patterns.

Present	Past
blow	
grow	
throw	
sing	
ring	
drink	
begin	
swim	
run	
give	
see	
hear	

Present	Past
feed	
meet	
creep	
keep	
sleep	
wear	
tear	
tell	
sell	
speak	
break	
shoot	

Present	Past
think	
fight	
buy	
take	
shake	
find	
wind	
rise	
write	
teach	
catch	
spend	

Time Filler:
Choose ten words from the list on page 48 and use each one in its own sentence. Keep coming back to these lists to check that you still know these useful words.

(2) Rewrite the sentences in the present tense (as if they are happening now).

I went to the beach and ate ice cream.

....

Ken hid inside a box and made no noise.

....

Pam did her homework and then sent it to the teacher.

....

(3) Change these verbs from present tense to past participle tense (has happened). These words usually follow "has," "have," "had," or "was." **Note**: A participle is a form of a verb.

Present	Past Participle
know	had ....
steal	had ....
fly	had ....

(4) Unscramble these letters to find four irregular verbs in the past tense.

dhel   ibtlu   meecab   rhotbug

....

More Prefixes

Try adding the prefixes
on these pages and make
a note of how they affect
the meanings of the words.

(1) Add **re-** or **pre-** to these root words.

.....build   ......pare   ......visit   .....play

.....write   ......dict   .....quest   .....move

(2) Connect the words that mean the opposite.

interior	concave
import	discord
convex	exterior
concord	export

(3) Complete this chart. For each prefix, write two more words.
Use a dictionary, if necessary.

Prefix	Example 1	Example 2	Example 3
a-	asleep		
be-	behind		
for-	forget		
pro-	progress		

(4) Underline the prefixes in these words.

hemisphere   hyperactive   infrared

postpone   ultraviolet   underarm

Time Filler:
How many words, with three or more letters, can you make with the letters in "recommendation"? Here are three words to get you started: "mention," "comet," and "train."

(5) Write the prefixes to complete these words.

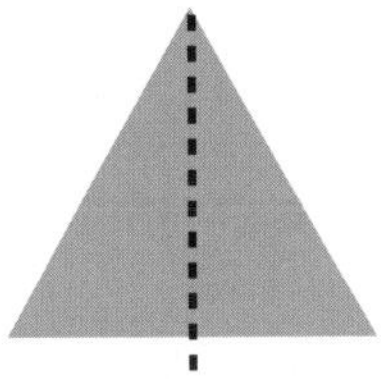

..........metry

..........circle

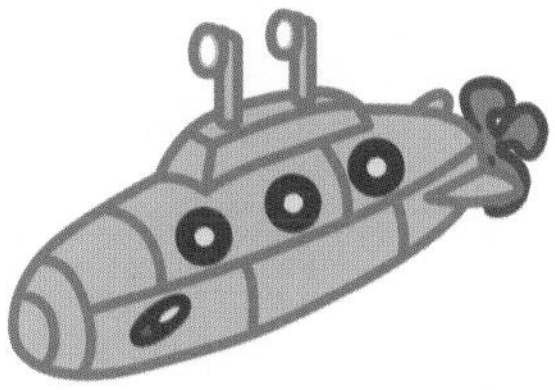

..........marine

(6) Find 12 words beginning with the prefixes **inter**-, **super**-, and **sub**- in this word search. Write the words you find in the chart below.

s	s	u	p	e	r	n	o	v	a	i
s	u	b	m	a	r	i	n	e	s	n
u	p	s	u	b	u	n	i	t	u	t
b	e	i	n	t	e	r	n	e	t	e
s	r	s	u	b	j	e	c	t	s	r
i	v	i	n	t	e	r	a	c	t	v
d	i	n	t	e	r	v	a	l	p	i
e	s	u	p	e	r	i	o	r	e	e
d	e	s	u	p	e	r	m	a	n	w

inter-	**super**-	**sub**-

Nouns or Verbs?

Adding a suffix can
change a root word into
a different part of speech.
Give these a try!

1 Nouns and adjectives can be changed into verbs using **-ate**, **-ify**, **-en**, and **-ize**. Write these words below. **Hint**: An **e** or **y** at the end of a root word has to be dropped.

elastic + ate = ...   note + ify = ...

length + en = ...   apology + ize = ...

2 Use the verb form of these words to complete the sentences.

deep   drama   beauty

The schoolchildren .... plays.

Models .... their faces by adding makeup.

Rivers .... when there has been heavy rain.

3 Verbs can be changed into nouns using **-tion**, **-ity**, and **-ness**. Complete these words. **Hint**: Use the spelling rules for consonant + **y** and root words ending in **e**.

reduce + tion = ...   creative + ity = ...

hard + ness = ...   happy + ness = ...

4 Change these words from verbs to either nouns or adjectives by removing or altering the suffixes.

solidify ....   quantify ....   fertilize ....

darken ....   loosen ....   activate ....

Time Filler:
Finding words within words helps learn spellings. For example, visualize a rat in "sepARATe" or an ass at the end of "embarrASS." Other ways to remember spellings is working out a phrase, such as: It is only natural to go Really Red and Smile Shyly when you are embaRRaSSed.

5 Some verbs get confused with other parts of speech and are tricky and troublesome to spell. Circle the verb in each pair of words and write the meaning of the other word. Use a dictionary to help.

affect   effect   ....

accept   except   ....

advice   advise   ....

6 Nouns and verbs that are spelled the same way are called homographs. A word's meaning depends on the stress and the way it is pronounced. Find the homographs in these sentences. Circle the verbs, and underline the nouns. **Hint:** Listen to the sound of each word.

The children present the thank-you present to their teacher.

The skipper lined up the oarsmen in a row and said, "Just row!"

The nurse wound a bandage around the wound.

I will invite you by sending you an invite.

Adding -**able** or -**ible**

Words with similar endings can be easily confused. There are some useful tips, but some words must be learned.

Words ending with -**able** or -**ible** are frequently confused.

(1) Often words ending in -**able** can be divided into two separate words. Write these words.

able to respect = ...   able to agree = ...

able to enjoy = ...   able to accept = ...

(2) Words that have **i** before the ending usually have -**able**. This ending is also often used after either a hard "c" or hard "g" sound. Add -**able** to complete these words.

reli............   soci............   amic............   navig............

(3) When -**able** is added to words that end in **e**, remember to drop the **e**. Write these words.

breathe + able = ...   value + able = ...

adore + able = ...   forgive + able = ...

(4) Words ending in -**ible** cannot be divided into two separate words. Write these words.

sens + ible = ...   terr + ible = ...

(5) Most words with **s** or **ss** in the middle end with -**ible**. It is also often used after a soft "c" or "g" sound. Add -**ible** to complete these words.

respons............   poss............   leg............   invinc............

Time Filler:
A way to remember "memorable" is by being "**able** to use your memory to remember to remove the **y**." Work out a way to remember the spellings of these words: "inevitable," "formidable," "resistible," and "flexible."

⑥ Follow the -**able** and -**ible** rules to work out the endings to these words, and then find them in the word search.

break‥‥‥‥ imposs‥‥‥ laugh‥‥‥‥

ed‥‥‥‥ pass‥‥‥‥ flex‥‥‥‥

vis‥‥‥‥ revers‥‥‥‥ envi‥‥‥‥

z	i	s	m	t	e	b	i	f	r
i	m	p	o	s	s	i	b	l	e
r	e	n	v	i	a	b	l	e	v
p	a	s	s	a	b	l	e	x	e
o	s	b	i	l	e	s	s	i	r
t	v	i	s	i	b	l	e	b	s
a	o	b	l	e	i	s	a	l	i
b	r	e	a	k	a	b	l	e	b
l	a	u	g	h	a	b	l	e	l
e	l	i	d	e	d	i	b	l	e

⑦ For words ending in -**ative** and -**itive**, consider the corresponding word ending in -**sion** or -**tion**. If the word ends in -**ation** use -**ative**, otherwise use -**itive**. Change each of these words.

competition ‥‥‥‥‥‥ affirmation ‥‥‥‥‥‥

information ‥‥‥‥‥‥ reproduction ‥‥‥‥‥‥

ie or ei?

I before **e** except after **c**
is a well-known rhyme,
but when does it apply?

(1) As you complete the words below, consider the rule:
i before **e** except after **c** or when the words say "ay"
like *neighbor* or *weigh*. (And a few other exceptions.)

rec__ve   th__f   rel__f
d__sel   c__ling   f__ld
p__ce   rec__pt   shr__k

(2) Complete these words, which have the "ay" sound.

fr__ght   __ght   n__ghbor
r__gn   v__l   w__gh

(3) This rule does not apply when using the plural form for words
ending in **cy**.

frequency   vacancy   policy
frequenc__s   vacanc__s   polic__s

(4) This rule does not apply when the letters **i** and **e** are pronounced
as separate vowels in words.

pric__r   sc__nce   soc__ty

(5) Here are some other exceptions to the **i** before **e** rule.

prot__n   s__ze   w__rd

Time Filler:
Remember that the word "for**ei**gn" is a foreigner that does not follow the **ie** spelling pattern, but a "fr**ie**nd" does. Make a list of words that follow the rule in your spelling journal (see page 5) and make a further column with words that are exceptions.

6 Can you find 10 words on page 56 in this word search?

r	e	d	s	e	i	e	w	c	s
e	r	e	c	i	e	v	e	i	l
c	p	i	i	c	t	h	i	e	f
e	o	s	e	i	z	e	g	l	w
i	l	e	n	w	s	c	h	i	e
v	i	l	c	f	e	i	f	c	i
e	c	f	e	i	l	d	e	n	r
p	i	w	i	e	r	i	h	g	d
r	e	t	c	l	p	e	i	t	l
s	s	i	e	d	i	e	c	s	e

Building Words

Knowing root words and how to add prefixes and suffixes to them helps to spell long words correctly. Are you ready? Let us get started!

1 Complete the chart with the long words made in each row. Keep the spelling rules in mind.

Prefix	Root	Suffix	Complete Word
con-	center	-ate	
ex-	peri	-ment	
de-	liver	-ance	
pro-	act	-ive	
ad-	vert	-ise	
inter-	nation	-al	
dis-	appear	-ance	
con-	grate	-ulate	

2 Knowing how words are related can help with spelling. Complete the root words.

Whole Word	Root Word
regularity	regul.....
opposite	opp......
conscience	sci........
definitely	fin....
government	gov......

3 Underline the root word in these words.

unbalanced   forgiveness   imprisonment

unlawful   reclaimable   forgetful

4 Underline both the prefixes and suffixes in these words.

irredeemable   adjoining   disposable

deflated   reappointment   projection

5 Choose a root word and a prefix and/or a suffix from the boxes to make 12 words.

Prefix	Root Word	Suffix
re-	take	-ive
im-	press	-ion
dis-	cover	-ment
mis-	prove	-ing
de-	break	-able
un-	agree	

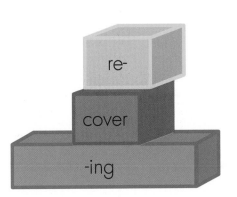

....

....

....

More Suffixes

Adding or altering a suffix can make the word a different part of speech, such as a noun, adjective, verb, or adverb.

Words ending in **-ant**, **-ent**, **-ance**, or **-ence** have rules to help you work out what parts of speech are.

1 The suffixes determine if words are adjectives or nouns. Give these columns of words a heading either adjectives or nouns.

importance	important		
distance	distant		
elegance	elegant		

evident	evidence		
violent	violence		
obedient	obedience		

What endings are used for adjectives? ....

What endings are used for nouns? ....

2 Change adjectives into nouns and nouns into adjectives in the charts.

Noun	Adjective
abundance	
magnificence	

Noun	Adjective
	defiant
	fragrant

3 The letters **t** and **v** are often followed with **-ance**. Complete the words.

accept..........   circumst..........   relev..........

4 Verbs ending in a vowel + **r** with a stress on the last syllable form nouns with **-ence**. Change these verbs into nouns.

differ..........   refer..........   rever..........

Time Filler:
"Necessary" is a tricky word to spell, but you can remember it by learning the phrase: When it is neCeSSary to dreSS nicely, choose a shirt that has one Collar and two Sleeves. Add any tricky-to-spell words on this page to your spelling journal (see page 5).

5 Some other noun endings are **-ency** or **-ancy** meaning the state of something. Change these adjectives into nouns.

emergent ....   irrelevant ....

constant ....   president ....

vacant ....   urgent ....

Words ending in **-ary** or **-ery** also cause confusion.

6 The ending **-ery** is less common and is usually only used in nouns. Complete these words.

batt.........   myst.........   machin.........

gall.........   cemet.........   monast.........   bak.........

7 The **-ary** ending is more common, so if in doubt use this ending. Complete these words.

Janu.........   Febru.........   diction.........   secret.........

libr.........   contr.........   necess.........   annivers.........

8 Use the words in question 7 to complete these sentences.

The first month of the year is ....

A .... can help to find the meanings of words.

It was .... for the teacher to cancel the school trip.

Hyphens

A hyphen is a linking mark between two or more words, but do you know when you should use it?

1 Use a hyphen when two words are used together as an adjective before a noun. Circle the compound adjectives.

A five-dollar bill   A trouble-free event

A full-length movie   A last-minute change

2 Use a hyphen when joining an adjective or noun to a past- or present-participle verb. Insert the missing hyphen.
Note: A participle is a form of a verb.

A sun dried tomato   A blue eyed doll   A hard wearing jacket

....

A well lit room   An old fashioned dress   A record breaking jump

....

3 Use a hyphen to make a group of words into an expression.
Link three words to make an expression.

do	go	one
happy	it	not
one	and	yourself
forget	to	white
black	me	lucky

Time Filler:
In your spelling journal (see page 5) include a list of hyphenated words that you have found in the books you have read. This will serve as a useful bank of words.

4 A hyphen is sometimes used to join a prefix to a word, especially if the prefix ends with a vowel and the root word begins with one. Correct these words.

coown ....   recreate ....   deenergize ....

5 A hyphen after a prefix also helps either to make the meaning of a word clearer or to change it completely. Put a hyphen after the prefix in each word and complete the sentence.

| resort | release | resign | recover | reform |

The artists .... their pictures.

The students .... the clay.

The postal workers .... the mail.

The woman decided to .... her apartment.

The ladies .... the chairs.

6 Some words started as two words, then were hyphenated, and are accepted as one word these days. Use a dictionary to find out if these words have a hyphen. Check if correct and put an X if incorrect.

rooftop ☐   sportswear ☐   highbrow ☐

racecourse ☐   nighttime ☐   roommate ☐

daytime ☐   saltwater ☐   newsstand ☐

Useful Word List 3

Read each column of words.
Next cover the words up one
by one and write them. Then
move on to the next column.

accommodate	....	exaggerate	....
analyze	....	familiar	....
ancient	....	foreign	....
appreciate	....	genuine	....
believe	....	government	....
celebrate	....	guarantee	....
challenge	....	haunt	....
committee	....	illustrate	....
correspond	....	influence	....
deceive	....	interrupt	....
definite	....	jealous	....
demonstrate	....	knuckle	....
embarrass	....	legend	....
especially	....	leisure	....

Time Filler:
Choose five words from this list
and use each one in its own sentence.
Keep coming back to these lists to check
that you still know these useful words.

lenient	....
lightning	....
majority	....
manufacture	....
mischievous	....
nuisance	....
occupy	....
origin	....
parallel	....
persevere	....
query	....
realize	....
recommend	....
rhyme	....

rhythm	....
scheme	....
severe	....
sincere	....
succeed	....
superior	....
thorough	....
triumph	....
umpire	....
variety	....
vocabulary	....
woolen	....
yacht	....
zero	....

Answers:

4–5 Syllables and Stresses
6–7 Origins of Prefixes

4

① Count the syllables in these words.

supermarket `4` gardening `3` furious `3`

adventure `3` preparation `4` journey `2`

② Link together the words that have the same number of syllables.

color   dangerous   picture   afterward

exhausted   shadow   introduce   outside

③ Look at the pictures of these two-syllable words. The second syllable has been given. Write the letters to spell the first syllable.

<u>trea</u>sure

<u>pre</u>sent

④ Look at the pictures of these two-syllable words. The first syllable has been given. Write the letters to spell the second syllable.

wi<u>zard</u>

whi<u>stle</u>

5

⑤ A part of each label is given. Look at each picture and complete its label. How many syllables does each word have?

volcano `3`   waterfall `3`   mountain `2`

⑥ When one syllable is longer and louder, it is a **stressed** syllable. Circle words that are stressed at the beginning, and cross out words that are stressed at the end.

~~demand~~   ~~restore~~   ~~forget~~   (table)   (famous)

⑦ These words are spelled the same, but have different meanings when the stress changes. For each word, put a check mark in the noun or verb column.

Word	Noun	Verb
record	✔	
re**cord**		✔
progress	✔	
pro**gress**		✔

Are the nouns stressed at the beginning or at the end?   Beginning

⑧ Write your name and circle the stress. How many syllables are there?
Answers will vary.

Once completed, this book will be a useful reference aid for the spelling rules. It will also provide tips for tackling tricky words and for making links between groups of similarly spelled words. These pages provide the first tip about breaking down words into smaller, more manageable chunks for each syllable.

6

① Complete this chart of prefixes that have come from the Latin language. For each prefix, use a dictionary to write two more words, and then work out their meanings. Answers may vary.

Prefix	Example 1	Example 2	Example 3	Meaning of Prefix
aqu-	aqueduct	aquatic	aquamarine	water
pro-	proceed	promote	progress	toward
im-	import	immerse	impact	into
in-, ir-, il-	incorrect	irregular	illiterate	not
pre-	preview	prepare	prevent	before
re-	redo	remake	rethink	again
sub-	submarine	subway	submerge	below
super-	superstar	superb	superhero	above
ex-	external	extinct	extract	out
co-	cowriter	cooperate	coequal	together
de-	defrost	destruct	depart	reversal

7

② Complete this chart of prefixes that have come from the Greek language. For each prefix, use a dictionary to write two more words, and then work out their meanings. Answers may vary.

Prefix	Example 1	Example 2	Example 3	Meaning of Prefix
anti-	antiviral	antidote	antisocial	against
auto-	autograph	automatic	autobiography	self
kilo-	kilogram	kilobyte	kilometer	thousand
cy-	cyclone	cycle	cylinder	circular
dyna-	dynasty	dynamic	dynamite	power
geo-	geography	geology	geosphere	Earth
micro-	microscope	microphone	microbiology	small
mis-	misbehave	mismanage	misinterpret	hate
peri-	periscope	peripheral	perimeter	around
mono-	monorail	monosyllable	monologue	one
bio-	biology	biodiversity	biography	life

Recognizing common prefixes helps children's word analysis skills, and knowing the meanings supports understanding as well as decoding words. This activity encourages children to use a dictionary to find related words and look at how the prefixes have affected the meaning.

Answers:

08–09 Root Words
10–11 Spelling Suffixes

8

(1) Complete this chart of Latin and Greek root words. For each root word, use a dictionary to write two more words based on this root word, and then work out its meaning. Answers may vary.

Root Word	Example 1	Example 2	Example 3	Meaning of Root Word
dict	dictate	dictation	dictionary	to say
pel	repel	expel	dispel	to drive
scrib	describe	prescribe	inscribe	to write
tract	attract	detract	retract	to pull
vert	divert	revert	invert	to turn
ject	eject	reject	project	to throw
chron	synchronize	chronology	chronicle	time
path	sympathy	pathetic	empathy	feeling
phon	telephone	microphone	symphony	sound
gram/graph	diagram	photograph	program	write or draw
scope	telescope	stethoscope	kaleidoscope	viewing instrument

Encourage children to first write down the words in the dictionary that are familiar to them. Then, have them write the words that they think might be useful for their reading and comprehension skills.

9

(2) The following words are French in origin:
Words with "sh" sound spelled **ch**, such as "chef;" words with "g" sound spelled **gue**, such as "tongue;" words with "k" sound spelled **que**, such as "unique."

Words with "s" sound spelled **sc**, such as "science," are Latin in origin. Words with "k" sound spelled **ch**, such as "chorus," are Greek in origin.

Say each of the following words aloud, and then write them under the French, Italian (Latin), or Greek flags.

chauffeur	chemist	fascinate	scissors
school	scene	chalet	antique
character	league	anchor	muscle

French
chauffeur
chalet
antique
league

Italian (Latin)
fascinate
scissors
scene
muscle

Greek
chemist
school
character
anchor

The Time Filler provides a strategy for learning spellings, for example, knowing that "fort" and "ate" are found in "fortunate."

10

(1) Complete this chart of common suffixes. For each suffix, use a dictionary to write two more words based on this suffix, and then work out their meanings. Answers may vary.

Suffix	Example 1	Example 2	Example 3	Meaning of Suffix
-ship	membership	relationship	friendship	state of office
-hood	childhood	parenthood	likelihood	condition
-ness	kindness	sadness	happiness	state of
-ment	enjoyment	statement	fragment	act of
-less	helpless	useless	airless	less of
-dom	kingdom	stardom	freedom	realm
-some	wholesome	awesome	handsome	tending to be
-craft	handicraft	woodcraft	craftiness	skill in
-ology	biology	zoology	geology	study of
-ward	downward	upward	forward	in direction of
-ism	criticism	realism	activism	belief in

Children should be familiar with many of these suffixes and this knowledge will help them spell words with these patterns in them. Page 11 also

11

(2) Make words by combining each word with one of the suffixes: **-ness**, **-ment**, or **-ship**. Remember: If the word ends in a consonant + **y**, change the **y** to an **i** before adding the suffix.

silly _silliness_   agree _agreement_   drowsy _drowsiness_

merry _merriment_   partner _partnership_   close _closeness_

(3) More than one suffix can sometimes be added. Write these words.

fear + some + ness = _fearsomeness_

care + less + ness = _carelessness_

(4) When the root word ends in **e**, the final **e** is dropped before adding the suffix. When the root word ends in **y**, the final **y** is dropped before adding the suffix. Complete the words in the chart with the vowel suffixes **-ive**, **-ic**, or **-ist**.

Suffix -ive	Suffix -ic	Suffix -ist
respons_ive_	horrif_ic_	violin_ist_
act_ive_	terrif_ic_	special_ist_
decorat_ive_	histor_ic_	art_ist_
narrat_ive_	allerg_ic_	journal_ist_

practices a few of the useful spelling rules regarding adding suffixes to root words ending in consonant + **y** and root words ending in the letter **e**.

Answers:

12–13 "le" Sound
14–15 Comparing Adjectives

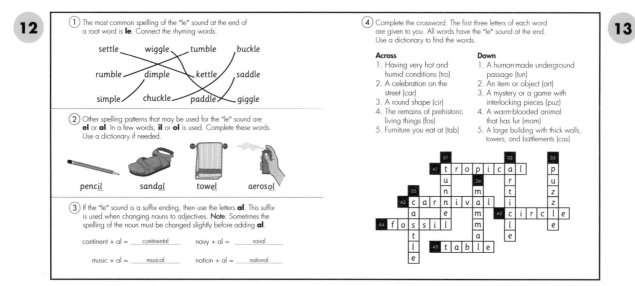

12

① The most common spelling of the "le" sound at the end of a root word is **le**. Connect the rhyming words.

settle   wiggle   tumble   buckle

rumble   dimple   kettle   saddle

simple   chuckle   paddle   giggle

② Other spelling patterns that may be used for the "le" sound are **el** or **al**. In a few words, **il** or **ol** is used. Complete these words. Use a dictionary if needed.

pencil   sandal   towel   aerosol

③ If the "le" sound is a suffix ending, then use the letters **al**. This suffix is used when changing nouns to adjectives. **Note:** Sometimes the spelling of the noun must be changed slightly before adding **al**.

continent + al = _continental_   navy + al = _naval_

music + al = _musical_   nation + al = _national_

13

④ Complete the crossword. The first three letters of each word are given to you. All words have the "le" sound at the end. Use a dictionary to find the words.

Across
1. Having very hot and humid conditions (tro)
2. A celebration on the street (car)
3. A round shape (cir)
4. The remains of prehistoric living things (fos)
5. Furniture you eat at (tab)

Down
1. A human-made underground passage (tun)
2. An item or object (art)
3. A mystery or a game with interlocking pieces (puz)
4. A warm-blooded animal that has fur (mam)
5. A large building with thick walls, towers, and battlements (cas)

Crossword answers:
- A1 tropical
- A2 carnival
- A3 circle
- A4 fossil
- A5 table
- D1 tunnel
- D2 article
- D3 puzzle
- D4 mammal
- D5 castle

The tricky thing about spelling with digraphs is figuring out which combination to use. There is often more than one option, as in the case of the "le" sound. Some children may recognize which spelling pattern to use by the visual shape of the word.

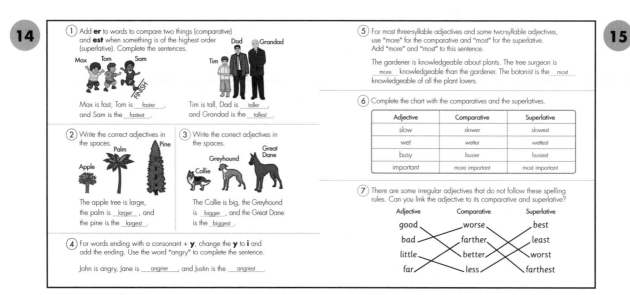

14

① Add **er** to words to compare two things (comparative) and **est** when something is of the highest order (superlative). Complete the sentences.

Max   Tom   Sam

Max is fast, Tom is _faster_, and Sam is the _fastest_.

Tim   Dad   Grandad

Tim is tall, Dad is _taller_, and Grandad is the _tallest_.

② Write the correct adjectives in the spaces.

Palm   Pine   Apple

The apple tree is large, the palm is _larger_, and the pine is the _largest_.

③ Write the correct adjectives in the spaces.

Greyhound   Great Dane   Collie

The Collie is big, the Greyhound is _bigger_, and the Great Dane is the _biggest_.

④ For words ending with a consonant + **y**, change the **y** to **i** and add the ending. Use the word "angry" to complete the sentence.

John is angry, Jane is _angrier_, and Justin is the _angriest_.

15

⑤ For most three-syllable adjectives and some two-syllable adjectives, use "more" for the comparative and "most" for the superlative. Add "more" and "most" to this sentence.

The gardener is knowledgeable about plants. The tree surgeon is _more_ knowledgeable than the gardener. The botanist is the _most_ knowledgeable of all the plant lovers.

⑥ Complete the chart with the comparatives and the superlatives.

Adjective	Comparative	Superlative
slow	slower	slowest
wet	wetter	wettest
busy	busier	busiest
important	more important	most important

⑦ There are some irregular adjectives that do not follow these spelling rules. Can you link the adjective to its comparative and superlative?

Adjective	Comparative	Superlative
good	worse	best
bad	farther	least
little	better	worst
far	less	farthest

Make sure children know that adjectives are used to describe more about a noun or pronoun. These pages practice the use of adding **er** and **est** to compare two, three, or more things. Often longer words sound awkward with these endings so "more" and "most" are used in front of them.

Answers:

16–17 "Not" Prefixes
18–19 Changing

16 | **17**

1. The prefix **in-** is used most often. Write these words.

not direct = indirect
not active = inactive
not accurate = inaccurate
not capable = incapable

2. Add **ir-** to root words beginning with **r**, making a double **r**. Write these words.

not regular = irregular
not responsible = irresponsible
not removable = irremovable

3. Add **il-** to root words beginning with **l**, making a double **l**. Write these words.

not legal = illegal
not legible = illegible
not logical = illogical

4. Add **im-** to some root words beginning with **m** and **p**. Write these words.

not mobile = immobile
not proper = improper
not possible = impossible

5. There are exceptions to the above rules. Circle the words spelled correctly.

(defrost) or infrost   irreasonable or (unreasonable)

illike or (dislike)   (depart) or inpart

(unload) or ilload   implease or (displease)

6. Find the opposite of each of these root words in the word search.

credible   aware   polite   code   order
accurate   patient   made   compose   modest

i	n	c	r	e	d	i	b	l	e
m	r	i	a	i	e	u	t	n	v
p	e	m	p	r	c	n	i	i	u
a	d	p	r	o	o	m	s	m	n
t	r	o	l	m	d	a	d	m	a
i	o	l	d	t	e	d	s	o	w
e	s	i	e	o	p	e	i	d	a
n	i	t	s	d	i	s	d	e	r
t	d	e	c	o	m	p	o	s	e
i	n	a	c	c	u	r	a	t	e

When deciding which prefix to use in question 6, children should first refer to the tips provided in the first four questions. If they are still unsure, they could try saying the word with each prefix and then thinking about which one sounds right. The word search will help to reinforce the pattern of the letters in the words.

18 | **19**

1. Add the letter **y** to these words and use the words to complete the sentences. **Hint:** For some short words, double the last consonant.

| crisp   fuss   sun   run   fur   full |

The bacon tasted crispy.   The day was hot and sunny.
The kitten was furry.   The toddler was fussy.
The gravy was runny.   The restaurant was fully booked.

2. These words end with an **e**. Add the letter **y** to them. **Hint:** Drop the **e** to add the **y**.

bone   smoke   stone   grease   laze
bony   smoky   stony   greasy   lazy

Why is the **e** removed?   The **e** is part of a digraph.

3. Circle the words with **y** as an "igh" sound. Cross out the words with **y** as an "ee" sound.

(cry)   boy   ~~bany~~   stay   ~~happy~~   (apply)

What is different about the **y** in the words not circled or crossed out?
The **y** is part of a diphthong, which is a two-vowel combination.

4. Can you find 10 words from page 18 in this word search?

h	a	b	m	r	h	o	t	b	y
u	n	o	n	l	a	z	y	m	g
r	u	n	n	y	p	a	l	p	r
r	o	y	u	a	p	p	l	y	e
y	m	g	l	p	y	d	n	f	a
b	f	u	l	s	a	f	n	o	s
p	u	f	z	y	l	u	s	s	s
z	s	m	o	k	y	l	a	g	l
l	s	f	r	m	f	l	r	r	t
o	y	t	g	s	s	y	t	f	m

Adding **y** to make the "ee" sound at the ends of words helps to make many adjectives. Point out to children that the rules for adding the suffix **y** are similar to those for adding other suffixes, such as **-ing**. Encourage children to list words with similar letter patterns in a spelling journal (see page 5) in order to make connections.

Answers:

22–23 Tricky Plurals
24–25 Silent Letters

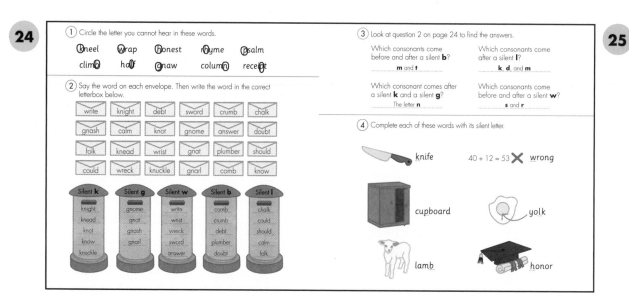

22

① Add **es** to words that end in **s**, **x**, **z**, **sh**, **ch**, or **ss** to make them plural.

brush — brushes   glass — glasses   match — matches

② For words ending in a consonant + **y**, change **y** to **i** and add **es**.

puppy — puppies   pony — ponies   city — cities

③ Add **s** to most words ending in an **o**.

piano — pianos   solo — solos   yo-yo — yo-yos

There are exceptions to this rule. Add **es** to make these words plural.

potato — potatoes   volcano — volcanoes   cargo — cargoes

④ For words ending in an **f** or **fe**, change **f** or **fe** to **v** and add **es**.

half — halves   leaf — leaves   knife — knives

There are exceptions to this rule. Just add **s** to make these words plural.

roof — roofs   chief — chiefs

⑤ For words ending in an **ff**, just add **s**.

cuff — cuffs   sniff — sniffs   puff — puffs

23

⑥ Some words change completely when made plural. Match each word to its plural.

child → children
mouse → mice
goose → geese
larva → larvae

⑦ Some words stay the same when made plural. Circle those words below.

(deer)   monkey   (sheep)   (fish)   cat

⑧ Complete the sentences using the plural of these words.

| penny | fox | loaf | foot |

Jan bought a candy with ten **pennies**.

In the field, a fox ran to join the other **foxes**.

The baker baked ten **loaves** of bread.

The plank of wood measured six **feet**.

By this stage, children will be aware that making plurals is not as simple as adding an **s** onto the ends of words. In these activities, some of the basic rules for making plural nouns are reinforced.

Exceptions to these rules are also explored. The Time Filler challenges children to consider applying the rules in a creative activity.

24

① Circle the letter you cannot hear in these words.

(K)neel   (W)rap   (H)onest   r(h)yme   (P)salm
climb   hal(f)   (G)naw   colum(n)   recei(p)t

② Say the word on each envelope. Then write the word in the correct letterbox below.

write	knight	debt	sword	crumb	chalk
gnash	calm	knot	gnome	answer	doubt
folk	knead	wrist	gnat	plumber	should
could	wreck	knuckle	gnarl	comb	know

Silent k: knight, knead, knot, know, knuckle
Silent g: gnome, gnat, gnash, gnarl
Silent w: write, wrist, wreck, sword, answer
Silent b: comb, crumb, debt, plumber, doubt
Silent l: chalk, could, should, calm, folk

25

③ Look at question 2 on page 24 to find the answers.

Which consonants come before and after a silent **b**?
m and **t**

Which consonant comes after a silent **k** and a silent **g**?
The letter **n**

Which consonants come after a silent **l**?
k, **d**, and **m**

Which consonants come before and after a silent **w**?
s and **r**

④ Complete each of these words with its silent letter.

knife   40 + 12 = 53 ✗ wrong

cupboard   yolk

lamb   honor

These questions challenge children to investigate words that have silent letters. Children will begin to see when they occur, and which letters are likely to be silent. These words need to be learned, but

these exercises support the memorization of the words. Encourage children to notice when silent letters appear in words, such as those mentioned in the Time Filler.

Answers:

26–27 Adding -ful and -ly
28–29 Apostrophes

26

① When the word "full" becomes the suffix **-ful**, the final **l** is dropped. Write each of these as one word.

full of truth = __truthful__   full of wonder = __wonderful__

full of cheer = __cheerful__   full of play = __playful__

② When words end in a consonant followed by **y**, change the **y** to **i**. (**Example:** pity + full = pitiful, but play + full = playful)

beauty + full = __beautiful__   plenty + full = __plentiful__

care + full = __careful__   power + full = __powerful__

③ The suffix **-ly** is added to an adjective to form an adverb. **Note:** An adjective describes a noun. An adverb describes an action.

quick + ly = __quickly__   slow + ly = __slowly__

④ If the root word ends in a **y**, then change **y** to **i**. Complete these words.

speedy + ly = __speedily__   happy + ly = __happily__

⑤ If the root words have a consonant + **le**, change **-le** to **-ly**.

gentle + ly = __gently__   simple + ly = __simply__

noble + ly = __nobly__   humble + ly = __humbly__

27

⑥ If the root word ends in **ic**, then add the letters **ally**. Change these words to adverbs.

basic __basically__   frantic __frantically__   dramatic __dramatically__

⑦ In some exceptions, just drop the **e**, then add **-ly** to the words.

true + ly = __truly__   whole + ly = __wholly__

⑧ Complete the chart below.

Adjective	Adverb		Adjective	Adverb
kind	kindly		easy	easily
quiet	quietly		heavy	heavily
strange	strangely		fateful	fatefully
famous	famously		noisy	noisily
normal	normally		loyal	loyally
general	generally		ready	readily

Write a sentence using one of the words from the chart.

__Answers will vary.__

These activities challenge children to use two frequently used suffixes to make adjectives and adverbs. Children may need reminding that the -**ful** suffix only has one **l**, even though it means "full of." The Time Filler gives children another fun strategy for reinforcing the spellings of tricky words.

28

① What are the missing letters in these words?

it's _i_   isn't _o_   they're _a_

I've _ha_   can't _no_   we'll _wi_

② Make these words into one word using an apostrophe.

I am __I'm__   he had __he'd__   do not __don't__

she would __she'd__   you will __you'll__   does not __doesn't__

③ Connect the words with their contractions.

should not ——— shouldn't
of the clock ——— o'clock
pick and mix ——— pick 'n' mix
are not ——— aren't

④ Rewrite the sentences in the speech bubbles, using contractions. Answers may vary.

I will not be there. — I won't be there.
It is not ready yet. — It's not ready yet.
Where has everyone gone? — Where's everyone gone?

29

⑤ An apostrophe is put after the owner's name to show something belongs to him or her. If the owner's name is a plural that does not end in **s**, then add an apostrophe and an **s**. Complete these words.

Tim's dog.   The women's group.

The dog's bone.   The children's game.

⑥ If the owner's name is singular but already ends in **s**, then still add an apostrophe and an **s**.

James's bat.   The actress's costume.

⑦ If the owner is plural and already ends in **s**, then just add an apostrophe.

The ladies' coat.   The dogs' collars.

Three years' work.   The two brothers' cars.

⑧ Sometimes contractions can be confused with possessives. Underline the correct word in the brackets for each sentence.

The children visited (they're/_their_) grandparents.

(_You're_/Your) going to be late for school.

(Who's/_Whose_) sweater is this?

The dog ate (it's/_its_) dinner.

These pages tackle both examples of when to use apostrophes: for contractions and for possessive nouns. If children need further support or are not confident, explain and practice each use separately. Other answers to question 4 are "I'll not be there." and "It isn't ready yet." Questions 6 and 7 explain when to add an apostrophe when the owner's name already has an **s**.

Answers:
30–31 Topic Prefixes
32–33 Doubling Letters

30

1. The prefix **auto-** means "self." Connect each word to its meaning.

autograph — A person's signature
automatic — Able to work by itself
autobiography — A person's story of his/her life

2. The prefix **circum-** means "round." What do each of these words go "round"?

circumference — Circle
circumnavigate — World

3. These words begin with the same prefix. The prefix means "distant." Circle the prefix.

(tele)phone   (tele)scope

4. What number do these prefixes mean?

cent- as in centipede 100   **tri-** as in tripod 3

quart- as in quarter 4   **pent-** as in pentagon 5

uni- as in unicycle 1   **dec-** as in decade 10

These challenges explore further prefixes that may appear in words used in children's other subjects, such as Math and Science. Knowing what the

31

5. Here are some words with the prefix **trans-**. What does it mean?

transmit   transfer   transport   translate   transplant

.... Across ....

6. The prefix **bi-** means "two" or "twice." Complete the crossword using **bi-** words. Use a dictionary to find the words.

Across
1. Two-footed
2. To split in two equal parts
3. Occurring every two years
4. Able to speak two languages

Down
1. Muscle with two starting points
2. Two-wheeled vehicle
3. Eyeglasses with two parts
4. Plane with two pairs of wings

Crossword answers:
A1. biped
A2. bisect
A3. biennial
A4. bilingual
D1. biceps
D2. bicycle
D3. bifocals
D4. biplane

prefixes mean, as well as their spellings, will help children's awareness of words with similar spelling patterns and links in meaning.

32

Complete these words following the doubling-letter rules.

1. When adding a suffix that begins with a vowel (**-ed**) to a word that ends with a vowel and a consonant, double the last consonant.

stop + ed = stopped   plan + ing = planning
fit + ed = fitted   step + ed = stepped

2. Double the last consonant of a word to add a suffix when the last syllable is stressed.

begin + er = beginner   occur + ing = occurring

3. Do not double the last consonant when a word ends in more than one consonant.

jump + ed = jumped   sing + er = singer
help + ing = helping   rest + ing = resting

4. Do not double the last consonant when the last syllable is unstressed.

offer + ed = offered   garden + er = gardener

5. Do not double the last consonant when the suffix begins with a consonant.

sad + ly = sadly   power + ful = powerful

33

6. Circle the words where the last consonant will be doubled before adding a suffix.

soak   (thin)   fast   pack   (spot)
(run)   walk   (plan)   clean   (sit)
comfort   disgust   (drop)   assist   forget
color   (grab)   enjoy   reason   listen

7. In the middle of a word, letters are doubled after a short vowel sound. Complete each word and connect it to its picture.

ra**bb**it   a**pp**le   ca**rr**ot   che**rr**y   pi**ll**ow

8. In the middle of a word, letters are not doubled after a long vowel sound. Circle the words with the long vowel sound.

dinner   (diner)   (super)   supper
(pole)   pollen   written   (writing)

These pages give two examples of when letters may be doubled in words: first, when adding suffixes to certain types of words, and second, after a short vowel in the middle of words. Children can refer to this page once completed. Encourage children to create rhymes for longer words with double letters.

Answers:

34–35 Crafty Consonants
36–37 Common Endings

34

① Say these words with the "k" sound aloud. Does the sound come at the beginning, in the middle, or at the end? Write the words in the chart.

keep   rocket   token   king   back   tank

Beginning	Middle	End
keep	rocket	back
king	token	tank

Does a vowel or a consonant go before the **k** at the end of a word?

A consonant

Write a word that rhymes with each of the words ending in the letter **k**.

Answers may vary.

② Say these words aloud. Does the letter **v** come at the beginning, in the middle, or at the end? Write them in the chart.

village   visit   five   develop   verb   river

Beginning	Middle	End
village	five	
visit	develop	
verb	river	

What do you notice about the chart?   _There are no words ending in **v**._

35

③ Underline the letter string **wa** in these words.

wa̲s   swa̲mp   wa̲tch   dwa̲rf   swa̲n

wa̲sp   swa̲rm   towa̲rd   rewa̲rd

Describe the sound of the letter **a**.

The sound is long and flat like a short "o" sound.

Using a dictionary, write two more words with the letter string **swa**.

Answers will vary.

④ Write the letter string **wo** in these words.

woman   swollen   word

worm   sword   two

swoop   awoke   wonder

How many words with the letter string **swo** are in your dictionary?

Answers will vary.

Does the letter string **wo** mostly come at the beginning or at the end of the word?

At the beginning.

Praise your child's efforts and achievements throughout this work and point out any mistakes in a positive, encouraging way. Even with an awareness of the various spelling rules, learning how to spell, and choosing which letters to use, is not always obvious. As a study aid, children could collect tricky words or similar words in a spelling journal.

36

① The most common spelling of "shun" is **-tion**. The root word usually contains a clearly pronounced vowel and is always a noun. Use these root words to complete the sentences below: subtraction, pollution.

The factory caused lots of _pollution_.

The problem 9 minus 8 is a _subtraction_ problem.

② Use **-cian** for the names of occupations. Write these words.

A person who does magic = _magician_

A person who plays music = _musician_

③ Use **-sion** after **r**, **l**, and sometimes **n**. Add **-sion** to these words.

version   propulsion   tension

④ Use **-sion** where the root word ends in **d**, **de**, **s**, or **se** and for a soft "sh" sound. Drop the root-word endings before adding the suffix to these words.

extend + sion = _extension_   confuse + sion = _confusion_

discuss + sion = _discussion_   possess + sion = _possession_

⑤ Use **-tion**, **-cian**, or **-sion** to complete these words.

position   passion   physician

education   optician   mission

37

⑥ The **-ient** is used after **t** or **c** to make the "shunt" sound. Add **-ient** to these words.

efficient   patient   ancient

⑦ The **-ial** ending is used after **t** or **c** to make the "shul" sound. The **-cial** ending often comes after a vowel and the **-tial** ending after a consonant. Add **-ial** to these words.

special   social   influential

⑧ The **-ure** ending is used after **t** to make the "chuh" sound or after **s** to make the "zhuh" sound. Complete these words.

moisture   measure   furniture

⑨ The **-ous** ending makes the "us" sound and is used for adjectives. Draw a line to link each word to its meaning.

anxious — describes a person who is worried
ravenous — describes an animal that is hungry
delicious — describes a meal that is tasty

⑩ If there is an "i" sound before the **-ous** ending, it is usually spelled as **i**, but a few words have **e**. Circle the correct word.

(serious) or sereous   hidious or (hideous)

These questions refer to some of the trickier spelling pattern endings in words. There are a handful of useful tips to help children remember them. If children are struggling to identify the correct spelling pattern, then encourage them to use strategies such as making phrases with the letters of the word or looking for words within the word.

Answers:

38–39 Homophones
40–41 Tricky Spellings

38

(1) Connect the words that sound the same.

peace   knot   plain   main   heard

mane   plane   herd   piece   not

(2) Write a sentence for each of the words "rode," "rowed," and "road."

Answers will vary.

Answers will vary.

Answers will vary.

(3) Put these words into the missing spaces to complete these sentences.

| heel | he'll | heal | too | two | to |

The runner's __heel__ had a blister.

__He'll__ need a bandage __to__ help it __heal__.

The runner had __two__ cuts on his leg, __too__.

(4) For each sentence, underline the correct word in parentheses.

Turn (<u>right</u>/write) at the intersection.

No one (new/<u>knew</u>) whose turn it was to do the dishes.

I can (<u>hear</u>/here) the birds singing.

39

(5) In the table below, write these words next to their meanings.

aloud   allowed   compliment   complement
descent   dissent   pair   pear
principal   principle   medal   meddle

Meaning	Word
Say out loud	aloud
Permitted	allowed
To make nice remarks	compliment
To make something complete	complement
Going down	descent
To disagree	dissent
The leader of a school	principal
A truth or rule	principle
Two things that go together	pair
A type of fruit	pear
An award	medal
To interfere	meddle

Practice activities about homophones show how words can sound the same, but are spelled differently and mean different things. These activities also demonstrate to children how careful and aware they need to be when writing homophones. Encourage children to use a dictionary to find the right words and check their answers.

40

(1) The spelling pattern **ou** makes the different sounds in these words: "out," "group," and "double." Join the groups of words with the same sound.

trouble   soup   house   found

shout   country   loud

cousin   coupon

boutique   young   route

(2) The spelling pattern **au** mostly makes an "aw" sound. Circle the words that make the "aw" sound.

(author)   (pause)   aunt   (sauce)

laugh   (haunt)   (launch)

What sound does the **au** pattern make in the words not circled? **Note:** This does not occur very often.

Short "a" sound

(3) Underline the letters that make the "ay" sound in these words.

v<u>ei</u>n   w<u>eig</u>h   <u>eig</u>ht   conv<u>ey</u>   ob<u>ey</u>

Is the "ay" sound in the words with letters **ey** stressed or unstressed?   Stressed

41

(4) The "ite" sound at the end of a word is mostly spelled with the pattern **ight**, but sometimes the letters **ite** or **yte** are used. Complete the words in these sentences with **ight**, **ite**, or **yte**.

Dan dressed in a wh<u>ite</u> sheet to give everyone a fr<u>ight</u>.

The computer had one megab<u>yte</u> left.

(5) The spelling pattern **ear** makes different sounds. Connect the words with the same sound.

appear   near   early

pear   wear   ear

rehearse   bear   Earth

(6) The letter string **ough** is tricky. Write each of the words in its rhyming group.

rough   tough   enough   cough   through   although   thought
bough   dough   trough   ought   bought   though

Rhyme with puff	Rhyme with toe	Rhyme with now	Rhyme with off	Rhyme with too	Rhyme with caught
rough	although	bough	cough	through	thought
tough	dough		trough		ought
enough	though				bought

Ask children to sound out the words as they complete them, so that they are connecting the spelling pattern with the sound used. Encourage children to write these words in their spelling journal. They can then add to each list as they come across new words in their reading and other language work.

Answers:

44–45 Verb Tenses
40–41 Soft Sounds

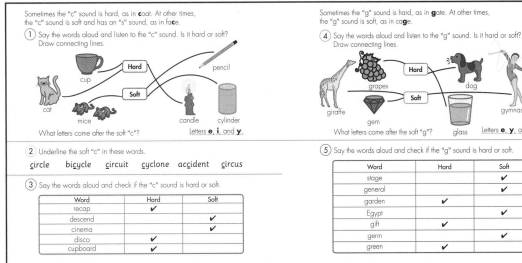

44

① Most words with short vowel sounds do not change when adding -**ed** or -**ing**.

help + ing = __helping__   ask + ed = __asked__

② For a word ending in **e**, drop the letter and replace it with either -**en** or -**ing**. Note: Some words may need to have consonants doubled.

come + ing = __coming__   drive + en = __driven__

ride + en = __ridden__   make + ing = __making__

③ For a word that has a short vowel before its final letter and a stress at the end, double the final letter and add either -**ed** or -**ing**.

swim + ing = __swimming__   hop + ing = __hopping__

refer + ed = __referred__   admit + ed = __admitted__

④ For a word ending with a vowel + **y**, just add -**ed** or -**ing**. If a word ends in a consonant + **y**, change **y** to **i** before adding -**ed**.

cry + ing = __crying__   reply + ed = __replied__

play + ing = __playing__   enjoy + ed = __enjoyed__

⑤ For words ending in **c**, add a **k**, and then add either -**ed** or -**ing**.

panic + ed = __panicked__   mimic + ing = __mimicking__

45

⑥ Add -**ing** and -**ed** or -**en** to each verb to tell what is happening now and what has happened before.

Verb	Happen**ing** Now (Add -**ing**)	Happen**ed** Before (Add -**ed** or -**en**)
look	looking	looked
walk	walking	walked
jump	jumping	jumped
write	writing	written
take	taking	taken
shop	shopping	shopped
drag	dragging	dragged
spy	spying	spied
carry	carrying	carried
hide	hiding	hidden

As children make various verbs while answering the questions, they should be aware of the **e** ending, the short vowel and consonant ending, the consonant and **y** ending, and the **c** ending. Discuss how the spelling rules are working on certain words to reinforce children's understanding so this can be applied for other words.

46

Sometimes the "c" sound is hard, as in **c**oat. At other times, the "c" sound is soft and has an "s" sound, as in fa**c**e.

① Say the words aloud and listen to the "c" sound. Is it hard or soft? Draw connecting lines.

Hard   Soft
cup   pencil   cat   mice   candle   cylinder

What letters come after the soft "c"?   Letters **e**, **i**, and **y**.

② Underline the soft "c" in these words.

_c_ircle   bi_c_ycle   _c_ir_c_uit   _c_y_c_lone   a_cc_ident   _c_ir_c_us

③ Say the words aloud and check if the "c" sound is hard or soft.

Word	Hard	Soft
recap	✔	
descend		✔
cinema		✔
disco	✔	
cupboard	✔	

47

Sometimes the "g" sound is hard, as in **g**ate. At other times, the "g" sound is soft, as in ca**g**e.

④ Say the words aloud and listen to the "g" sound. Is it hard or soft? Draw connecting lines.

Hard   Soft
giraffe   grapes   gem   dog   gymnast   glass

What letters come after the soft "g"?   Letters **e**, **y**, and **i**.

⑤ Say the words aloud and check if the "g" sound is hard or soft.

Word	Hard	Soft
stage		✔
general		✔
garden	✔	
Egypt		✔
gift	✔	
germ		✔
green	✔	

Investigating the hard and soft "c" and "g" sounds will help children to listen out for the soft sound and not to be caught out by the spelling. For the soft "c" sound, children are likely to use the letter **s**, and for the soft "g" sound, they use the letter **j**. Explain to children that they should look out for the letters **e**, **i**, and **y** that come after the soft sounds.

Answers:

48–49 Irregular Verbs
50–51 More Prefixes

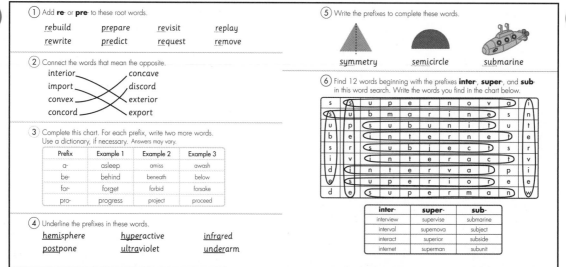

48

1. Change these words from present tense (happening now) to past tense (already happened). Use a dictionary if needed. Look out for spelling patterns.

Present	Past	Present	Past	Present	Past
blow	blew	feed	fed	think	thought
grow	grew	meet	met	fight	fought
throw	threw	creep	crept	buy	bought
sing	sang	keep	kept	take	took
ring	rang	sleep	slept	shake	shook
drink	drank	wear	wore	find	found
begin	began	tear	tore	wind	wound
swim	swam	tell	told	rise	rose
run	ran	sell	sold	write	wrote
give	gave	speak	spoke	teach	taught
see	saw	break	broke	catch	caught
hear	heard	shoot	shot	spend	spent

49

2. Rewrite the sentences in the present tense (as if they are happening now).

I went to the beach and ate ice cream.
..........I go to the beach and eat ice cream.........

Ken hid inside a box and made no noise.
..........Ken hides inside a box and makes no noise..........

Pam did her homework and then sent it to the teacher.
..........Pam does her homework and then sends it to the teacher..........

3. Change these verbs from present tense to past participle tense (has happened). These words usually follow "has," "have," "had," or "was." **Note**: A participle is a form of a verb.

Present	Past Participle
know	had __known__
steal	had __stolen__
fly	had __flown__

4. Unscramble these letters to find four irregular verbs in the past tense.

dhel	ibtlu	meecab	rhotbug
held	built	became	brought

Verbs that do not follow any spelling pattern rule need to be learned and used confidently. Throughout this stage, children will be progressing to become aware that there are verbs that

completely change when moving from tense to tense. If used incorrectly in their speech, repeat the sentence with the correct usage so that these irregular verbs can be reinforced.

50

1. Add **re**- or **pre**- to these root words.

__re__build   __pre__pare   __re__visit   __re__play
__re__write   __pre__dict   __re__quest   __re__move

2. Connect the words that mean the opposite.

interior   concave
import   discord
convex   exterior
concord   export

3. Complete this chart. For each prefix, write two more words. Use a dictionary, if necessary. Answers may vary.

Prefix	Example 1	Example 2	Example 3
a-	asleep	amiss	awash
be-	behind	beneath	below
for-	forget	forbid	forsake
pro-	progress	project	proceed

4. Underline the prefixes in these words.

__hemi__sphere   __hyper__active   __infra__red
__post__pone   __ultra__violet   __under__arm

51

5. Write the prefixes to complete these words.

__sym__metry   __semi__circle   __sub__marine

6. Find 12 words beginning with the prefixes **inter**-, **super**-, and **sub**- in this word search. Write the words you find in the chart below.

s	u	p	e	r	n	o	v	a	l	n
s	u	b	m	a	r	i	n	e	s	n
u	p	s	u	b	u	n	i	t	u	t
b	e	i	n	t	e	r	n	e	t	e
s	r	s	u	b	j	e	c	t	s	r
i	v	i	n	t	e	r	a	c	t	v
d	i	i	n	t	e	r	v	a	l	p	i
s	u	p	e	r	i	o	r	e	e
d	e	s	u	p	e	r	m	a	n	w

inter-	super-	sub-
interview	supervise	submarine
interval	supernova	subject
interact	superior	subside
internet	superman	subunit

These final pages of prefixes cover some more of the ones that children may frequently use, such as **re**-, **pre**-, **inter**-, and **pro**-. The Time Filler activity can be played with any word and could be done as

a competition between members of the family to see who can find the most words with extra points for the person with the longest word.

Answers:

52–53 Nouns or Verbs?
54–55 Adding -able or -ible

52

1) Nouns and adjectives can be changed into verbs using **-ate**, **-ify**, **-en**, and **-ize**. Write these words below. **Hint**: An **e** or **y** at the end of a root word has to be dropped.

elastic + ate = __elasticate__   note + ify = __notify__

length + en = __lengthen__   apology + ize = __apologize__

2) Use the verb form of these words to complete the sentences.

| deep   drama   beauty |

The schoolchildren __dramatize__ plays.

Models __beautify__ their faces by adding makeup.

Rivers __deepen__ when there has been heavy rain.

3) Verbs can be changed into nouns using **-tion**, **-ity**, and **-ness**. Complete these words. **Hint**: Use the spelling rules for consonant + **y** and root words ending in **e**.

reduce + tion = __reduction__   creative + ity = __creativity__

hard + ness = __hardness__   happy + ness = __happiness__

4) Change these words from verbs to either nouns or adjectives by removing or altering the suffixes.

solidify __solid__   quantify __quantity__   fertilize __fertilization__

darken __dark__   loosen __loose__   activate __activity__

53

5) Some verbs get confused with other parts of speech and are tricky and troublesome to spell. Circle the verb in each pair of words and write the meaning of the other word. Use a dictionary to help.

(affect) effect   "Effect" means a result of an action.

(accept) except   "Except" means excluding something.

advice (advise)   "Advice" means a recommendation.

6) Nouns and verbs that are spelled the same way are called homographs. A word's meaning depends on the stress and the way it is pronounced. Find the homographs in these sentences. Circle the verbs, and underline the nouns. **Hint**: Listen to the sound of each word.

The children (present) the thank-you _present_ to their teacher.

The skipper lined up the oarsmen in a _row_ and said, "Just (row)"

The nurse (wound) a bandage around the _wound_.

I will (invite) you by sending you an _invite_.

These pages explore how nouns and verbs can be created by adding suffixes and prefixes or changing the stress on words. After children have completed these questions ask them to think of other words they may know as examples for each one.

54

Words ending with **-able** or **-ible** are frequently confused.

1) Often words ending in **-able** can be divided into two separate words. Write these words.

able to respect = __respectable__   able to agree = __agreeable__

able to enjoy = __enjoyable__   able to accept = __acceptable__

2) Words that have **i** before the ending usually have **-able**. This ending is also often used after either a hard "c" or hard "g" sound. Add **-able** to complete these words.

reliable   sociable   amicable   navigable

3) When **-able** is added to words that end in **e**, remember to drop the **e**. Write these words.

breathe + able = __breathable__   value + able = __valuable__

adore + able = __adorable__   forgive + able = __forgivable__

4) Words ending in **-ible** cannot be divided into two separate words. Write these words.

sens + ible = __sensible__   terr + ible = __terrible__

5) Most words with **s** or **ss** in the middle end with **-ible**. It is also often used after a soft "c" or "g" sound. Add **-ible** to complete these words.

responsible   possible   legible   invincible

55

6) Follow the **-able** and **-ible** rules to work out the endings to these words, and then find them in the word search.

breakable   impossible   laughable

edible   passable   flexible

visible   reversible   enviable

z	i	s	m	t	e	b	i	i	l	f
i	m	p	o	s	s	i	b	l	e	e
r	e	n	v	i	a	b	l	e	v	e
p	a	s	s	a	b	l	e	x	e	e
o	s	b	i	l	e	s	s	i	r	r
t	v	i	s	i	b	l	e	b	b	s
a	o	b	l	e	i	s	a	l	l	i
b	r	e	a	k	a	b	l	e	e	b
l	a	u	g	h	a	b	l	e	e	l
e	l	i	d	e	d	i	b	l	l	e

7) For words ending in **-ative** and **-itive**, consider the corresponding word ending in **-sion** or **-tion**. If the word ends in **-ation** use **-ative**, otherwise use **-itive**. Change each of these words.

competition __competitive__   affirmation __affirmative__

information __informative__   reproduction __reproductive__

These exercises provide some of the tips to consider when deciding whether to use **-able** or **-ible**, and **-ative** or **-itive** at the ends of words. Crosswords and word searches are useful exercises for helping children become familiar with the patterns of letters in words. Children may wish to design their own with their tricky spellings.

Answers:

56–57 **ie** or **ei**?
58–59 Building Words

56

① As you complete the words below, consider the rule:
i before **e** except after **c** or when the words say "ay"
like *neighbor* or *weigh*. (And a few other exceptions.)

rec**ei**ve	th**ie**f	rel**ie**f
d**ie**sel	c**ei**ling	f**ie**ld
p**ie**ce	rec**ei**pt	shr**ie**k

② Complete these words, which have the "ay" sound.

fr**ei**ght	**ei**ght	n**ei**ghbor
r**ei**gn	v**ei**l	w**ei**gh

③ This rule does not apply when using the plural form for words
ending in **cy**.

frequency	vacancy	policy
frequenc**ie**s	vacanc**ie**s	polic**ie**s

④ This rule does not apply when the letters **i** and **e** are pronounced
as separate vowels in words.

pric**ie**r	sc**ie**nce	soc**ie**ty

⑤ Here are some other exceptions to the **i** before **e** rule.

prot**ei**n	s**ei**ze	w**ei**rd

⑥ Can you find 10 words on page 56 in this word search?

r	e	d	s	e	i	e	w	c	s
e	r	e	c	i	e	v	e	i	l
c	p	i	i	c	t	h	i	e	f
e	o	s	e	i	z	e	g	l	w
i	l	e	n	w	s	c	h	i	e
v	i	l	c	f	e	i	f	c	i
e	c	f	e	i	l	d	e	n	r
p	i	w	i	e	r	i	h	g	d
r	e	t	c	l	p	e	i	t	l
s	s	i	e	d	i	e	c	s	e

57

This common known rhyme is helpful up to a point
as it is only applied when words contain the "ee"
sound. The practice on page 56 helps children to
be aware of the many exceptions to this rule,
including plurals and when vowels are
pronounced separately in words.

58

① Complete the chart with the long words made in each row.
Keep the spelling rules in mind.

Prefix	Root	Suffix	Complete Word
con-	center	-ate	concentrate
ex-	peri	-ment	experiment
de-	liver	-ance	deliverance
pro-	act	-ive	proactive
ad-	vert	-ise	advertise
inter-	nation	-al	international
dis-	appear	-ance	disappearance
con-	grate	-ulate	congratulate

② Knowing how words are related can help with spelling.
Complete the root words.

Whole Word	Root Word
regularity	regular
opposite	oppose
conscience	science
definitely	finite
government	govern

③ Underline the root word in these words.

un**balanced**   for**giveness**   im**prison**ment

un**lawful**   re**claim**able   for**get**ful

④ Underline both the prefixes and suffixes in these words.

<u>ir</u>redeem<u>able</u>   <u>ad</u>join<u>ing</u>   <u>dis</u>pos<u>able</u>

<u>de</u>flat<u>ed</u>   <u>re</u>appoint<u>ment</u>   <u>pro</u>ject<u>ion</u>

⑤ Choose a root word and a prefix and/or a suffix from the boxes
to make 12 words. Answers may vary.

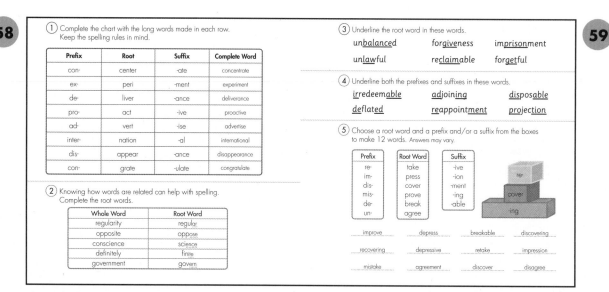

Prefix	Root Word	Suffix
re-	take	-ive
im-	press	-ion
dis-	cover	-ment
mis-	prove	-ing
de-	break	-able
un-	agree	

improve	depress	breakable	discovering
recovering	depressive	retake	impression
mistake	agreement	discover	disagree

59

These challenges show how words can be built up
in parts. Continue to encourage children to reverse
this process when spelling longer words by splitting
the words into smaller chunks to make them more
manageable. These can be split by syllable chunks
as well as by prefix, root word, and suffix as
practiced on these pages.

Answers:

60–61 More Suffixes
62–63 Hyphens

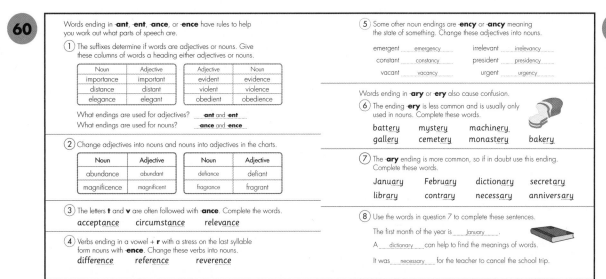

60

Words ending in **-ant**, **-ent**, **-ance**, or **-ence** have rules to help you work out what parts of speech are.

① The suffixes determine if words are adjectives or nouns. Give these columns of words a heading either adjectives or nouns.

Noun	Adjective	Adjective	Noun
importance	important	evident	evidence
distance	distant	violent	violence
elegance	elegant	obedient	obedience

What endings are used for adjectives? **-ant** and **-ent**
What endings are used for nouns? **-ance** and **-ence**

② Change adjectives into nouns and nouns into adjectives in the charts.

Noun	Adjective	Noun	Adjective
abundance	abundant	defiance	defiant
magnificence	magnificent	fragrance	fragrant

③ The letters **t** and **v** are often followed with **-ance**. Complete the words.

accep**tance**   circums**tance**   rele**vance**

④ Verbs ending in a vowel + **r** with a stress on the last syllable form nouns with **-ence**. Change these verbs into nouns.

differ**ence**   refer**ence**   rever**ence**

61

⑤ Some other noun endings are **-ency** or **-ancy** meaning the state of something. Change these adjectives into nouns.

emergent ___emergency___   irrelevant ___irrelevancy___
constant ___constancy___   president ___presidency___
vacant ___vacancy___   urgent ___urgency___

Words ending in **-ary** or **-ery** also cause confusion.

⑥ The ending **-ery** is less common and is usually only used in nouns. Complete these words.

battery   mystery   machin**ery**
gallery   cemetery   monastery   bakery

⑦ The **-ary** ending is more common, so if in doubt use this ending. Complete these words.

January   February   diction**ary**   secret**ary**
libr**ary**   contr**ary**   necess**ary**   annivers**ary**

⑧ Use the words in question 7 to complete these sentences.

The first month of the year is ___January___.

A ___dictionary___ can help to find the meanings of words.

It was ___necessary___ for the teacher to cancel the school trip.

Children practice making links by identifying how spellings of words relate to each other in their various forms. For example, if children know how to spell "important" then they can make the connection to use the **-ance** spelling pattern for the noun.

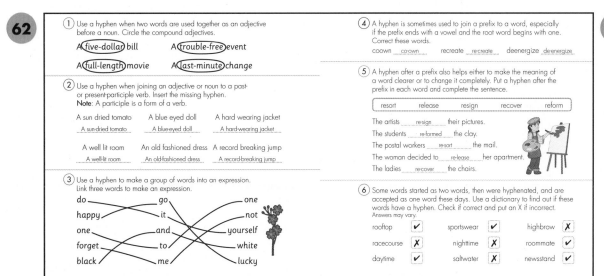

62

① Use a hyphen when two words are used together as an adjective before a noun. Circle the compound adjectives.

A (five-dollar) bill   A (trouble-free) event

A (full-length) movie   A (last-minute) change

② Use a hyphen when joining an adjective or noun to a past- or present-participle verb. Insert the missing hyphen.
Note: A participle is a form of a verb.

A sun dried tomato   A blue eyed doll   A hard wearing jacket
A sun-dried tomato   A blue-eyed doll   A hard-wearing jacket

A well lit room   An old fashioned dress   A record breaking jump
A well-lit room   An old-fashioned dress   A record-breaking jump

③ Use a hyphen to make a group of words into an expression. Link three words to make an expression.

do — go — one
happy — it — not
one — and — yourself
forget — to — white
black — me — lucky

63

④ A hyphen is sometimes used to join a prefix to a word, especially if the prefix ends with a vowel and the root word begins with one. Correct these words.

coown ___co-own___   recreate ___re-create___   deenergize ___de-energize___

⑤ A hyphen after a prefix also helps either to make the meaning of a word clearer or to change it completely. Put a hyphen after the prefix in each word and complete the sentence.

| resort | release | resign | recover | reform |

The artists ___re-sign___ their pictures.
The students ___re-formed___ the clay.
The postal workers ___re-sort___ the mail.
The woman decided to ___re-lease___ her apartment.
The ladies ___re-cover___ the chairs.

⑥ Some words started as two words, then were hyphenated, and are accepted as one word these days. Use a dictionary to find out if these words have a hyphen. Check if correct and put an X if incorrect. Answers may vary.

rooftop	✔	sportswear	✔	highbrow	✗
racecourse	✗	nighttime	✗	roommate	✔
daytime	✔	saltwater	✗	newsstand	✔

Children should be aware of how the use of a hyphen can affect the meaning of a word or a phrase. These exercises practice when hyphens are used. When writing a hyphen, it should not be confused with a dash, which is longer. The answers to question 6 may vary depending on the dictionary children are using.

Answers:
Useful Words
to Learn to Spell

The method of learning how to spell using the look, say, cover, write, and check method is a familiar practice for many children. Encourage children to re-read the lists of words from pages 20–21, 42–43, and 64–65 on a frequent basis and test them until they are confident when spelling them accurately in

their writing. Each time, praise their progress and improvement. For any spellings that are causing difficulty, suggest creating phrases or finding words within words as practiced in some of the Time Fillers. Add them to their spelling journal as a reference as well.

Monday	winter	fifteen	bicycle	junior	situate	familiar	parallel
Tuesday	spring	sixteen	breathe	knowledge	sufficient	foreign	government
Wednesday	summer	seventeen	building	library	sure	genuine	persevere
Thursday	fall	eighteen	certain	material	though	guarantee	query
Friday	January	nineteen	conscience	medicine	through	haunt	realize
Saturday	February	twenty	continue	nephew	accommodate	illustrate	recommend
Sunday	March	thirty	describe	occasion	analyze	influence	rhyme
holiday	April	forty	dictionary	often	ancient	interrupt	rhythm
yesterday	May	fifty	difficult	opposite	appreciate	jealous	severe
tomorrow	June	sixty	early	particular	believe	knuckle	sincere
birthday	July	seventy	Earth	peculiar	celebrate	legend	succeed
anniversary	August	eighty	excite	position	challenge	leisure	superior
weekend	September	ninety	extreme	possess	committee	lenient	thorough
weekly	October	hundred	grammar	punctuate	correspond	lightning	triumph
tonight	November	thousand	guard	quarrel	deceive	majority	umpire
today	December	million	heart	quarter	definite	manufacture	variety
month	eleven	accident	immediate	recite	demonstrate	mischievous	vocabulary
morning	twelve	advertise	increase	regular	embarrass	nuisance	woollen
afternoon	thirteen	approve	independent	reign	especially	occupy	yacht
season	fourteen	benefit	injure	separate	exaggerate	origin	zero